JUST FRICKIN PICK ONE

HOW TO OVERCOME SLOW DECISION MAKING, STOP OVERTHINKING ANXIETY, LEARN FAST CRITICAL THINKING, AND BE DECISIVE WITH CONFIDENCE

REESE OWEN

CONTENTS

ALL BOOKS BY YOURS TRULY

I'm a very busy, very prolific writer.

In fact, I have so many books about getting your ish together and living your best life, that I have a website:

ReeseOwenBooks.com

Look, Ma, I made it!

Check out my other ebooks, paperback books, and audiobooks available on Amazon and Audible.

B*TCH DON'T KILL MY VIBE:

How To Stop Worrying, End Negative Thinking, Cultivate Positive Thoughts, And Start Living Your Best Life

JUST DO THE DAMN THING:

How To Sit Your @ss Down Long Enough To Exert Willpower, Develop Self Discipline, Stop Procrastinating, Increase Productivity, And Get Sh!t Done

MAKE YOUR BRAIN YOUR B*TCH:

Mental Toughness Secrets To Rewire Your Mindset To Be Resilient And Relentless, Have Self Confidence In Everything You Do, And Become The Badass You Truly Are

Chill Out, Bro:

How To Freak Out Less, Attack Anxiety, Calm Worry, & Rewire Your Brain For Relief From Panic, Stress, & Anxious Negative Thoughts

INTRODUCTION

You're sweating. No—you are *drenched* with sweat. Everything is in slow motion. A distant sounding echo-y voice fades in from the background. It feels like a movie, but this is your real life. The stakes are real. This is it. This is the moment everything has been building up to. You know your heart is racing, but it feels like it's beating in slow motion. The sound of your heartbeat magnifies. It's so loud you can't even hear your own thoughts anymore. Everything is a blur. All you can focus on is what's directly in front of you. There are people all around you. Their faces come into focus. Everyone is looking at you. Counting on you. It's all up to you. The distant sounding, muffled voice finally becomes clear. It sounds annoyed, and puts space in between each word deliberately as if it assumes you're deaf or don't speak English.

"Do you want a small fry or a medium fry?"

The man behind the register stares at you blankly.

Still not knowing what to say, you turn around, as if to seek guidance from a stranger.

You lock eyes with a group of children at a nearby table, and their gaze darts away quickly as they go back to eating their burgers, pretending they didn't see you.

The girl behind you in line rolls her eyes at you, noticing your apparent struggle.

"Are you going to be okay?" she asks.

You don't know how to answer. *Are* you going to be okay? If you get the small fry, you could still be hungry afterwards, so instead of going to catch the tail end of that networking event you were planning on going to, you'd go home to eat Cheetos to supplement your insufficient small fries. And in doing so, you'd miss out on meeting your would-be business partner and love of your life at the networking event. If you get the medium fry, you could begin a habit of overeating, your body could all of a sudden need more calories to satisfy it, your insatiable appetite would get out of control, you'd become obese, then they'll make a TLC show about the sad downturn of your life. Your arteries will clog and your cholesterol will shoot up. Then you'll die of a heart attack before you can see your children walk down the aisle. You don't have or want children, but still.

You still can't decide. People are looking at you. They're judging you. You'll never be able to live this down or set foot in this place again. But this is your favorite restaurant. You'll have to move. The humiliation will force you to abandon your friends and family and go to a new city, where no one knows you...and where they don't sell fries. You'll die of loneliness...and potassium deficiency from not eating enough potatoes. What do you do??

Can we all just take a moment to agree that making decisions is freaking hard?

Oftentimes, we're so intimidated by the prospect of picking something that we just don't pick anything at all and we remain stuck in a state of mental (and sometimes physical) paralysis. We hate being put on the spot, and under pressure, we end up deciding on things we don't even want. Sometimes, you just pick something, *anything*, just so the mental agony will be over. Then, our struggle with choosing bleeds over from the important to the unimportant, and all of a sudden, *everything* is hard. One day, we are struggling with a really challenging decision like whether or not we should take a new job that has a serious pay cut but great benefits and better potential to grow, and the next day, we are struggling on deciding between a cheeseburger or a nugget meal at the drive-thru window. What's up with that?

It's like the more pressure we put on a decision, no matter its true magnitude, the harder any and every decision becomes, and it all becomes life or death. Then this causes us to second guess our logic, doubt our discernment, and ultimately lose faith and confidence in ourselves. Our minds feel muddled and our judgment feels clouded. We feel incapable and don't trust ourselves to choose something that's in our best interest. Then fear sets in as we become afraid of being put on the spot to have to make a decision going forward. Before we know it, we are totally screwed because we cannot for the life of us decide if we want to wear blue or green underwear that day, so we are sweating bullets over our underwear drawer trying to figure out what on earth we are going to do with our lives.

Or maybe you are lucky enough to actually be able to come to a decision. But then instead of doing all your doubting and second guessing on the front end, you just do all your doubting and second guessing on the backend. You seemed confident when making the decision, but now that it's made, you beat yourself up and drive yourself crazy wondering if it was in fact the right choice. Now you've developed a fear of commitment. We can be seemingly confident on the outside, but be anything but on the inside.

Have you ever beat yourself up over the amount of trouble you have with making choices? *"Like, come on dude, one or the other, it's not that freaking hard. Just make a decision and go with it already!"* This is a pretty common reality for many people who struggle with making decisions and committing to their choice, no matter how seemingly large or small the decision is. Realize that you are not alone and that sweating, pit of your stomach, sick feeling that you get every single time you are faced with a decision that you need to make is actually completely normal. Fun, no. But normal, yes. Functional, no. But normal, yes. Helpful, unh-uh. But normal, yes.

In fact, the fear of making decisions is so common that

psychologists have literally coined a phrase for it: "aboulomania," which means "pathological indecisiveness." Your difficulty making decisions is likely not a mental illness (even though it can feel like it sometimes), yet the fact that they have essentially created a mental-illness term relating to this phenomenon is evidence enough that many people are dealing with it, not just you. So allow that to make you feel a little bit better about your plight.

But just because you are not the only one who struggles with this does not mean that staying in a chronic state of indecisiveness is a good idea. Just because it's normal, doesn't mean you shouldn't do anything to fix it. It's not exactly something they give out trophies for, and if they did, I doubt it would have a place on your mantle. Being a totally horrible decision maker is nothing to be proud of, as I am sure you already know, and it is likely something that you are more than ready to kick seeing as how you have this book. In order for you to destroy your crappy decision-making once and for all, you'll need to start equipping yourself with better skills. That's right—decision making is a skill. And as with any skill, it can be learned, practiced, and mastered.

If you are ready to stop clenching your butt and grinding your teeth every time the waitress asks you if you want another glass of water, this book is for you. You are going to learn how to get out of your own way and exercise effective problem-solving skills so that you are no longer being annihilated by questions like, "Do you want fries with that?" or "Will you marry me?" Being able to make decisions is critical for anyone who is looking to kick ass in the game of adulting and finally start making choices that they feel good about.

In school, they taught us how to figure out the area of a triangle and how to know the part of speech of a word in a sentence, but did no one think that maybe we should learn about how to make decisions? Considering the fact that we make 35,000 decisions every single day according to PsychologyToday.com, it seems like decision making would be a skill worth teaching in school. When was the last time you came across 35,000 triangles you needed to find the area of in a single day? That's what I thought.

In doing a little digging as to why this type of information is not taught in formal education settings, the general consensus was that decision-making skills are believed to be natural byproducts of the curriculum that we were being taught. Like, because I learned how to decipher when it was appropriate to use a calculator and when I should just go with my mental math skills, I should also automatically know how to choose a life partner? What a load of crap.

What's in this book is what they *should* have been teaching us in school rather than falsely assuming that these vital life skills were being learned as byproducts of those ridiculous assignments they had us doing in fourth-period class. But that's okay. We'll pick up where school left off. In this book, we'll cover some of the science behind decision making, why it's so hard, mental shifts to reframe and bring sense to the process of decision making, and actions you can implement to make it easier. And you'll walk away with a toolkit that you can use to make future decisions both great and small, and the confidence to commit to your decisions and not second guess yourself. And as a free bonus, I'll throw in a sense of comfort in assuring you that everything is going to be okay.

I have to put a pretty important disclaimer in here before you get going, though, you know, so you don't come back and freak out on me for what you are about to see. In this book, you may find some a-ha's, but you are also going to find some common sense, which means that some of what you learn here may not necessarily be new information to you, but for whatever reason, you still haven't been able to implement it to your benefit in your life. I'm hoping with this book that I can change that for you. But remember, the process of making decisions is supposed to be simple, so that you can actually do it. You have to do this 35,000 times a day, so it can't be too complicated. So don't kick the messenger when you realize how easy this actually is.

The good news is, you're not completely doomed. I mean, you were able to at least come to the decision to get this book, so you're not totally hopeless. But this book works best if you do, which means it's going to require you to take action. A lot of people don't like this part. They like to read self-help books as if they're entertainment. Let's not forget here that self-help is about helping yourself. That means you're going to have to actually do something, to actually *change* something. That something that you have to do is going to be different, uncomfortable, and difficult compared to what you're used to doing, whether it's an action, a thought, or a belief system. And that something that you're going to have to change is you. So don't just go through this book nodding your head at the parts you like, rolling your eyes at the parts you don't, or furrowing your brow over the parts you think you already know.

Do something about it. Do something different. If you want to actually help yourself, you have to force yourself to do things differently and think differently even though your brain is going to try to scream you back into your comfort zone every time you try to make a change. In times like this, it can be helpful to remember why it's so important to you to make a change in the first place. Armed with strong reasons for why you need to make a behavioral or belief shift even though it feels like it sucks in the moment, will help give you the mental strength and willpower needed to push through and stick with your new choices and ultimately reap the benefits of having a new life. It'll give you the fuel you need to see things through.

So let's dive in so you can gain some mental clarity and start making decisions with confidence and boldness so you'll no longer find yourself quivering because the cashier asked whether or not you want a receipt for your order. It's time to yank your head out of the sand once and for all and start making decisions like you mean it. It's time to just frickin pick one.

CHAPTER 1

WHY YOU NEED TO PICK QUICK

BEING indecisive can be a real pain in the ass, and if you are not dealing with it, you are going to find yourself being the biggest nuisance to yourself. I mean, the only thing worse than the mental torture of not being able to decide one way or the other, is all of the horribly annoying symptoms that go along with indecisiveness—the anxiety, the guilt, the fear, the butt sweat, and the weird looks from people around you...decision limbo sucks.

Decisiveness Has Its Benefits

Think of what a relief it would be to no longer invest so much of your energy into every single point of decision. And the worst thing about it is that it doesn't even matter the size of the decision. No matter how big or small a choice is that you may want or need to make, having a hard time actually making that choice will leave you susceptible to increased feelings of stress and overwhelm, which don't exactly make it easier for you to choose.

In fact, the more mental or emotional duress you are under when making a decision, the more likely it is that you'll end up with a less than savory outcome. And the more that you experience this difficulty with deciding, the smaller of decisions it will take to put you into a complete tailspin. So you're not just going to find yourself hung up on the big things, you'll find yourself getting snagged on smaller and smaller issues. And the added stress you experience will make it harder for you to properly give your attention to anything beyond the particular decision at hand. So not only will you be suffering from mental turmoil from the decision itself, but it will also cause an inability to focus or think clearly that will make it a struggle for you to get through your regular day-to-day.

Emotionally and mentally, being decisive means you get to skip out on fatigue caused by your brain being constantly consumed with stress. A person who is mentally clear and free of unnecessary stress generally experiences lower cortisol and adrenaline production, which means that their body is going to be functioning more optimally. See, in small doses, cortisol and adrenaline increases can be beneficial to your body, but for someone who is constantly under stress and pressure, this can become problematic when we start getting into long term stress. Long term stress levels have been linked to everything from increased risk of mental ailments like anxiety and depression, to physical ailments like heart disease and increased risk of heart attacks.

Physically, being decisive means that you are being protected from the stress that indecisiveness can bring with it. The more your mind is working with and for you, the more relaxed and the healthier your body will be. Keeping your stress in check by just freaking picking something already and committing to that is a great way to make sure that you are keeping your body in an optimal mental and physical state. Plus, you get to build your trust and confidence in yourself. And you get the mental matter off your plate, so your brain can be free to do other things.

Indecisiveness is not only going to take your stress levels through the roof, but it is also going to decrease your abilities and even your credibility in many ways. Not only are you putting additional stress on yourself, but you're also putting added stress on the people around you. You don't want to be that person who no one can stand being around because you can't make even the simplest of decisions. And that's if you even have people to be around. Decision is about commitment. And a fear of deciding is a fear of commitment. This can bleed into your personal relationships and have an adverse effect on your life.

You don't want to become *that* friend. You know the one. The one who is in their late twenties or thirties and they have yet to accomplish anything because they cannot make up their freaking mind and go for it already. The one who's always declining social invitations because they can't afford the gas to get there, or the one who loves to show up to every social invitation, yet their wallet never seems to make an appearance because they never decided on or landed a decent paying job. So far, they have no committed relationship, no career, no fixed address, and very few accomplishments to show for their lives because they simply cannot decide what it is that they want and how they want to get it.

There's a good chance that they're not only living a mediocre life with little to show for anything they've ever done, but that they're also making up lame ass excuses as to why. Like, instead of admitting they don't have a decent career and financial status because they can't pick one thing and stick with it, they blame the economy, the current sitting president, the great wealth divide, income inequality, climate change...they point the finger at everything except themselves. Or, instead of admitting that they couldn't decide on what they wanted out of a relationship, which in turn causes all their potential partners to flee the scene and scatter like cockroaches when you turn the lights on, they claim that all of these people have something wrong with them or they just "don't get them the way a life partner should."

See, being indecisive leads to you being that person: that person who not only has a blank page for a life resume, but that person who has to come up with lame excuses that everyone can see through because it helps you feel better about being totally shitty at making decisions. People who are indecisive not only experience greater levels of stress within themselves, but they can also experience greater levels of repercussions from the people around them because they come across as being incapable of deciding and committing to something.

Being decisive means that once you make a decision, you can commit to it and start to see the benefits. Decisions are often tied to actions. And those actions can have a positive benefit in our lives. There may be an unexpected financial benefit as well. No more buying expensive gym memberships only to go for the first week and then quit because you cannot decide to get your ass out of bed and actually make it to the gym. See? It literally pays to be decisive and to actually stick to your decisions.

The Importance Of Timeliness

Part of being decisive is not just learning how to make a decision, but it is learning how to make a decision *fast*. Listen, that barista that just asked you if you want a grande or a venti mocha does not have six hours for you to draw up a pros and cons list, make a Venn diagram, conduct a survey, put together a PowerPoint, make a spreadsheet to analyze the data, and consult with your mentor. So if you take six hours to decide which size coffee to get, I'm sorry, that doesn't count as you being decisive just because you *finally* made a decision. Likewise, that date you are sitting across from? Their stomach is growling and they are sick of waiting all night for you to decide on what you want to order, and they're starting to wish they'd swiped left. Life choices get a lot harder than this, my friend. You're going to have to do better. Good decision making means that you take an amount of time to make a choice that is appropriate and proportionate to the gravity of the potential repercussions of that choice. So when it comes to the little things in life (which is most things), that means you're going to have to hurry it up, buddy.

Learning how to pick quick is both for you and for the

people around you. The faster you can make a choice, the faster you can all move forward with your lives. People who are trash at making decisions hold the flow back, which leads to everyone feeling frustrated and totally bummed out from the slowness of *you*. As you learn how to make decisions faster, not only do you get what you want faster, but also, the people around you can actually stand to be around you. Win win. I mean, think about it, are you going to want to keep hanging out with a person who cannot ever for the life of them make up their freaking mind about anything? Probably not. You are likely going to find them to be annoying, difficult to be around, and challenging to be patient with.

Ever had your plans fall through because you could never come up with one?

It's been a long week, and it's finally the weekend. You've got your sights set on hanging out with your friend and you've been talking about it all week. But then...

"What do you want to do?"

"I don't know, what do you want to do?"

"I don't know, what do you want to do?"

On and on forever until the other person questions their decision to choose you as a friend and regrets the day they ever met you. So what do you end up doing instead of spending time with your friend, which you were looking forward to all week? Watching that same C-level sitcom on Netflix...alone...again. Surely, this is getting old for you.

You don't want your relationships to suffer because of your snail's pace decision making. And you definitely don't want it to prevent you from having a relationship in the first place. If you come across someone who wants to date you, if you make up your mind quickly to just give it a shot and go on a date with them, then you stand the chance of having a wonderful experience with this person and even potentially falling in love. But if you spend too much time ruminating over it and don't make up your mind, your Prince or Princess Charming is going to go find someone else, and boom—there goes your happily ever after.

Think Fast, Profit Faster

Let's talk about something that makes the world go round. No, I'm not talking about love. No, I'm not talking about the gravitational pull of the sun coupled with conservation of angular momentum. I'm talking about money. Friends, family, the potential love of your life, mental health, emotional stability, ability to sleep at night...these are not the only things at stake here. If that's not enough motivation for you to once and for all become a quicker picker, let's take a look at your wallet for a minute. If it's empty, you're going to be glad you found this book.

We all know about the stock market. But we don't all take advantage of it—sometimes not at all, and sometimes, not at the right time. Well-known and respected entrepreneur Gary Vaynerchuck famously says that his decision to not invest $25,000 in Uber when it was a little fledgling startup cost him a cool 500 mil. That's what his initial 25K investment would be worth today—500 million dollars.

Considering that Gary's net worth is $160 million, that's not *too* hard a pill to swallow, but an extra 500 million dollars in the bank wouldn't exactly be hurting him either.

That's a very pricy decision.

Stockbrokers have to decide every day what to buy, what to sell, when to buy, when to sell. And the market is literally changing every minute of every hour of every day. If they don't make decisions quickly, that could mean a huge loss. And if they do make decisions quickly, and those decisions end up being the right decisions, they could be in for a huge windfall.

Ok, so maybe you're not the Wolf of Wall Street, and you're thinking—tell me about something that's actually relevant to me. And in response to that, I would say stock market investing is a part of every fiscally responsible person's balanced asset portfolio. And *then* I would say you're not getting ahead at work either without being decisive and being quick about it.

Employers value people who can make decisions. Are you tired of living paycheck to paycheck and want to finally get to drive a car that doesn't look like it came out of a junkyard or a salvage auction? That's going to require more money. And if you're in the working world, that's going to mean a promotion and a raise. When you are decisive, people see you as being level-headed, wise, intelligent, and qualified, which leads to them trusting you more. The more you can be trusted when it comes to your decision-making skills, the more you are going to be look at as an authority.

People who are more decisive are valued more by bosses because they are known for being effective at seeing pros and cons quickly, weighing options, and executing plans, which to the company they work for, means turning more profits. If it's a promotion you're after, it's going to require you to in some way be an effective leader. And what's the foundation for leadership? Decisiveness. If you want to catch the attention of your boss, you've got to learn to pick quick.

If you are looking to go for a leadership or management role, learning how to become decisive and quick with your decision-making skills is a necessary art that you are going to need to master. After all, have you ever met a leader who lead their team into battle by saying, "Okay, fire now! Wait, not yet! Okay, now! Nope, one sec! This way! Never mind, that way!" No. You've never met them because they zig-zagged themselves and their team straight into death. And that's no way to get promoted. Decision making does not exactly come naturally to everyone. For most people, it is a learned quality that they realize they need in order to advance. Or at least to order coffee at a cafe. Plus, being decisive at work means that you're going to be able to get your job done quicker and move through challenges with greater ease, which means making the time between 9 and 5 go by a lot quicker and more pleasantly.

But this does not just go for the corporate world though, either. If you are one of those folks who have thrown up your metaphorical (or literal) middle finger at the corporate world and chosen to go your own path, this applies to you too. The entrepreneur is in the driver's seat.

If you're an entrepreneur, decisiveness is just as critical—perhaps even more so. You can't steer the ship in any meaningful direction without choosing which way to turn the damn wheel. It is solely up to you to call the shots. A failure to do so is a failure to run your business well...or even at all, really.

In the world of business, there is a term known as opportunity cost—that is, essentially the cost of missing an opportunity. This term is usually brought up when comparing making one choice over another. But when it comes down to it, making no choice is a choice too. And making no choice over another also illustrates the principle of opportunity cost. And it's not just for business, either. It can be applied to any part of your personal or professional life, really, whether you're a CEO or not. Not making a decision...whether it's to take advantage of a new business opportunity, say yes to that person who asks you out, get a personal trainer, sign the lease on that new place...these all have opportunity cost tied to them. By not doing them, you could be missing out on the potential benefits those opportunities could have yielded you.

Speaking of opportunity, there's another way being decisive can pad your wallet. Let's not forget about the added bonus of being able to cut down your spending by simply taking advantage of special offers before they end. We've all seen the deals: 50% off, act now! But you didn't act now. You stood there like you were cryogenically frozen in time, so you missed out and you're paying double because of it. If you want to fatten up your wallet, you need to do whatever it takes to become decisive *and* timely with your decisions. Don't analysis paralysis your way to bankruptcy.

But quick decisions don't just mean more money. People who are capable of making decisions and committing to them find themselves profiting quickly and also recovering from losses quickly. If something doesn't work out, they're quick to just make a decision to pivot and try something else, and they're on the road to recovery a heck of a lot faster than the guy who can't just freaking decide.

CHAPTER 2

WHY YOU CAN'T DECIDE

THE REALITY IS: making decisions is not as simple as it should be, and unfortunately, there are actually several elements at play that contribute to making it harder than we think it ought to be. Understanding the basics behind why you cannot for the life of you choose one way or the other will give you insight into why your brain is a total wreck whenever you are faced with a metaphorical fork in the road. Then, armed with the behind the scenes knowledge, you can consciously combat these phenomena when they're at work. So let's break things down a little bit more.

The fundamental reason behind why decision making is so hard is actually ridiculously straightforward. Believe it or not, you do not actually suck at making decisions, nor is your brain intentionally working against you to prevent you from choosing between hot coffee or iced coffee, or staying with your long-term partner or leaving them. It is not like there is some weird center in your brain that says, "Ha-ha, let's see how much I can screw with them before they notice!" In fact, there is no center in your brain that is misfiring at all when you find it to be insanely challenging to make a choice for yourself. What is actually happening is that you are experiencing that thing that seems to be the root of all life's problems and issues—fear. And come decision time, that fear is triggering your fight or flight response.

When you are faced with a choice that you need to make, you immediately begin to look into your memory bank to help you choose. Your memories help you identify times in the past where you had to make a similar selection in an effort to accumulate enough information to help you decide which way you should choose in the present moment. Say you are at the movies, and the concession stand attendant asks you if you want butter on your popcorn. You would immediately begin to go into your memory bank, remember a time when you had butter on your popcorn, and a time when you did not, and you would likely choose the time you preferred most. If you enjoyed the popcorn with the butter more, then you would likely choose to have butter on your popcorn this time. Simple. Easy peasy.

Decision making becomes challenging, however, when your memories show you that there is a high chance that you could experience something negative if you decide one way or the other. For example, say you are in need of more money, and you want to ask your boss for a promotion at work so you can start earning a higher salary.

Perhaps you know that you are a great fit for the promotion, you're confident that you have shown this to your boss, and you feel like you can easily qualify. In your mind, there is no reason why you should not be considered or why you would be turned down because you know that you have what it takes and that your boss likes you aplenty. Yet, for some reason, you are having a hard time asking.

The root of that difficulty asking for something you know you deserve is that you are afraid of rejection or of something equally as uncomfortable taking place. Despite you knowing that you are qualified, chances are, you are remembering a time in the past where you asked for something equally as important to you, and you were shot down. Maybe, in addition to being shot down, you were even ridiculed and treated poorly for even wanting or merely expressing interest in what you asked for. So not only did you feel bad for being rejected, but you also felt bad because of what was said about you. Fast forward to now, and your fear of making a decision to go talk to your boss is natural because you do not want to face that same degree of shame or discomfort again.

In a scenario like the one above, having difficulty making a decision makes total sense. We do not want to experience something negative, so we choose to avoid making the decision altogether so that we do not experience anything at all. No, we do not get to experience the upside of a promotion and a raise. But that's not what we're thinking about in that moment. All we're focused on is that we do not have to experience the rejection we fear will result if we ask, and we also do not experience the disappointment in ourselves. So we stay in limbo and pretend that we are still in the decision-making phase so we don't have to feel bad about ourselves.

And that points to a weird little thing about human nature —we are more motivated to protect ourselves from loss than we are to propel ourselves towards gain. This behavioral concept is called loss aversion in the field of cognitive psychology. To the irrational human mind, it's better to not lose 20 bucks than it is to gain 20. As it translates to our behavior, we would sooner do something to keep ourselves from losing something, than we would do something that would result in us gaining something. That's why it's so hard to do the things you need to do in the first place. But that's a tangent for another book.

Instead of going down that rabbit hole, allow me to share something that illustrates this idea. Certain companies take advantage of the idea of loss aversion and use it as a way to motivate their salespeople. You would think that if you offered a salesperson an incentive, they would want to work towards it. If you provide a BMW to a salesperson for a certain amount of sales, you'd think that dangling carrot would be enough to drive performance. But it was found that if you flip that idea around, and give the salesperson the BMW in the beginning, they'll work harder to not lose it, and *that* turned out to be the better driver of performance. Why are we talking about BMWs in a book about decision making? The point here is that, if you apply the concept of loss aversion to decision making, you can see that when you boil it down, when a decision comes down to picking between losing or gaining, we'd rather not take the risk of loss, so our decision will reflect that.

In easier situations, like ordering something from a restaurant or choosing whether you want to buy the blue sweater or the brown sweater, it may not make as much sense as to why this would matter so much. Surely, a small thing such as this could not bring a great deal of loss, disappointment, rejection, or negativity into our lives, could it? No, probably not, but that doesn't always stop it from feeling that way. Chances are, if you order a meal that you do not particularly like, you are not going to feel a deep sense of embarrassment or shame around your choice.

Likewise, if you buy the brown sweater and realize later that you may have liked the blue one more, you'll probably get over it pretty quickly. Yet, still, you will feel some degree of negativity around your choice. Maybe you will engage in some negative self-talk where you say "I knew I should have gotten the other one" or "I never pick the right things," and so you start bullying yourself over the choice you made.

Of course, the amount of negative self-talk or disappointment that you engage in will likely be disproportionate to the event itself, yet still, you engage in it anyway. At this point, you are so filled with fear around making the wrong choice that you start second-guessing yourself or feeling doubt every time you need to pick between this or that, since you've bullied yourself into such a big fear of letting yourself down. In the bigger picture, you simply learned a lesson for next time, but in your mind, you are a total screw up. Naturally, this type of behavior makes the decision process feel even more negative and pressuring, which means that you are going to be even less likely to want to decide next time because you won't want to put up with the name-calling and the constant reminders of your flaws and shortcomings. If you wanted that, you could just go to your Aunt Margaret's house.

In an ideal world, decisions would be made by carefully considering all of the information presented before us, and making a rational, well-thought-out choice based on our findings. Oh—and that choice wouldn't take us five and a half centuries to come to. We would have a quick and easy time comparing our options and picking the one that serves our needs the most. We would rarely run into problems with decision making because we'd be able to easily and cleanly choose what is best.

Unfortunately, there are so many different variables that come into play, making it harder for us to commit to a choice and carry through with it. We find ourselves unwilling to decide one way or another because our emotions, fears, thoughts, opinions, and uncertainty all lead to us feeling like we could not possibly make a wise decision at any given moment. These variables can all cause us to feel like we do not have enough information to make a choice one way or the other, or feel like we're stuck at an impasse, even if the choice we ought to make seems glaringly obvious.

The way you automatically make decisions varies depending on who you are and what process you have come to favor for yourself. Typically, when faced with two options, people begin to think about two things: what they want and what other people want. That's when the beads of sweat come in and they begin to panic. Why? Because more often than not, what they want and what other people want *for them* are two different things. So they find themselves frustrated because they want to be happy with their decision, but they do not want others to be disappointed with it, or disappointed with them for making it. So, they remain trapped in a state of indecisiveness and discomfort.

If making choices in a healthy and ideal manner, however, a person would start every decision by deciding what their goal is and what its value is to them. For example, if you wanted to order lunch, you would first decide that your goal is to eat something. In your head, you can hear your mother's voice on repeat, constantly telling you to eat your vegetables so you don't become one. But also in your head, are mouthwatering flashbacks from Food Network's *Man vs Food*. So you need to clarify if your goal is to eat something healthy or tasty. You decide on healthy.

Next, you would determine the value of your goal, and how important it is to you. Is it absolutely necessary for your meal to be healthy for you? Do you *really* want that thigh gap and a future life free of hypertension and diabetes? Or is it more important to you to have a taste-bud orgasm from that double bacon cheeseburger with barbecue sauce and onion rings?

After you decide your goal and the value of your goal to you, you would start looking at your options and simply pick the one that is going to be most likely to help you reach your goal. After your decision is made, you would evaluate it to see how the outcome was and determine whether or not it would be a good decision for you to make again in the future. Now, you have information in your memory bank to help you make similar choices in the future.

So that's how the decision-making process would be if it were easy and straightforward. But as mentioned earlier, there are many variables that make this whole thing easier said than done. Some of the major obstacles that can get in the way and derail your decision-making process include feelings, instincts, intoxication, and external sources. Each of these can throw you for a loop and cloud your judgment.

If you are being clouded by feelings, your brain is just trying to make you feel good. It's addicted to that dopamine. You may find yourself wanting to avoid the right decision for fear of it making you feel discomfort or pain, or you may find yourself wanting to choose the wrong decision because you know that it will bring instant gratification in the immediate or near future. The problem with the feeling part of your mind is that it can often bring you into your primal senses, which means that you will not necessarily be thinking in terms of what is the right decision logically. When we make decisions based on our emotions, we fail to look at the bigger picture, which often leads to making the wrong decision long-term. As a result, we may feel a small sense of comfort or relief in the now, but we will feel disappointment, resentment, or regret in the long run when we realize that our decision was impulsive and not well thought out when it comes to our overall best interest.

If you are being clouded by your instincts, this indicates that you are likely failing to make a decision because your gut is telling you that whatever it is that you are leaning towards is the wrong choice. There's a time and a place for gut instinct, but you have to remember that your gut works closely with your emotions, so if you are feeling afraid, your gut is going to tell you "no" or prompt you to make the less scary decision because, to your body, your very life is at stake. When it comes to literal survival, gut instinct can serve you in helping you choose not to turn left and walk down that dark alley towards the man in the ski mask with the switchblade in his hand. But the trouble comes in with non life-threatening situations that are perceived or treated as life-threatening. The thing is: nearly everything good in life is on the other side of fear, outside of your comfort zone. So listening to your initial gut instincts can rob you of amazing experiences, connections, and growth opportunities because those instincts of yours are going to interpret the normal fear and discomfort that inevitably comes with confronting something new and different as being a threat to your wellbeing. So if your life isn't truly at stake, realize that your instincts are likely going to give you the wrong information when it comes to making a decision.

If you are intoxicated...I mean...do I even have to tell you?

Your judgment is being clouded because you are not presently able to think with a clear frame of mind. People who are intoxicated frequently choose the instant-gratification choice. Beyond the instant-gratification factor, most people who are intoxicated also struggle to see all of the facts and information, so they find themselves not fully informed on what it is that they are deciding. While this may not be such a big deal when you are deciding if you want a #1 or a #2 from the fast food restaurant after the club closes, it can be a very big deal when you are trying to decide whether or not it is a good idea to drive your vehicle or go home with a stranger at the end of the night.

Lastly, external influences can have a huge impact on the choices we make. Our judgment can be clouded by having other people weighing in with their opinions by telling us what they think is right or wrong for us. *I don't want to move to Boise and carry on the family legacy and be a podiatrist, Dad!* Sorry, I had a moment.

But, that's the struggle. When it comes to people that we either love or trust in any way, we will find ourselves having a challenging time making the right choice for ourselves because we may trust this other person to be able to make the right decision for us. As a result, if their choice and our choice are not aligned, and we trust them, we may feel obligated or inclined to choose in favor of their decision and not our own, which can result in us making the wrong decision for ourselves.

CHAPTER 3
PSYCHOLOGY 1. YOU 0.

WHEN IT COMES to your sucky decision-making skills, if we take a look at the scoreboard, Psychology is in the lead. We can break it down to three main issues: cognitive bias, the paradox of choice, and the simple fact that you are probably not using your brain. Yes, that last one could sound a little harsh, but if you own it, you'll develop the ability to get inside your head and make the old thinker actually work for you instead of against you for a change.

Cognitive Bias Has You Beat

What is cognitive bias, exactly? It's a tendency towards a particular pattern of thinking that is very commonly studied in the world of psychology. It sounds fancy, but it can be explained pretty easily. To put it simply, a cognitive bias is basically a piece of personal information that influences your individual judgment about various things in life. Not all cognitive biases will impact your decision-making skills negatively, but some will, so it is important to understand what they are and how they impact you.

A great example of a common cognitive bias that many people have that impacts their decision-making skills is known as confirmation bias. Confirmation bias is a form of cognitive bias that essentially puts people into the frame of mind that leads them to believe that the information they already know is true and anything else is false. This is the reason why if you present someone with information that contradicts what they already believe to be true, they start aggressively protecting their existing beliefs. And if you're not careful, or if you really strike a nerve, things can escalate real quick.

Their aggressive protection of their beliefs is less about them genuinely believing that they are right, and more about them genuinely not wanting to admit that they may be wrong. We see this often in the social media space when keyboard warriors come out, fingers blazing on a subject they are overly passionate about, and they continue to defend their opinion even after hundreds, thousands, millions, or billions of other people (scientists included) have provided them with evidence that they are wrong. (*Ah-hem, flat earth...*) Instead of seeking to explore the bigger picture, a person who is actively using confirmation bias will only look for information that validates their existing opinion so that they do not have to restructure their belief system. So when it comes to making choices, they will be more inclined to choose not what's best, but what's already in line with their deep rooted beliefs.

Another type of cognitive bias that people use is known as the halo effect, which affects people's judgment by causing them to want to see things in the same light, always. This is why they say positive first impressions are huge. If you leave a positive impression on someone, they have a strong tendency to continue to see you in that positive light. Even if you happen to do something negative or something that calls your character into question, they will likely try and justify it in a way that allows them to continue seeing you in a positive light. Why? Quite frankly, processing conflicting information is challenging and takes up a lot of mental resources. From a mental laziness standpoint, it's always easier to defend your opinion instead of change it. The trouble with this is that it can lead to us giving unfairly positive evaluations to people who don't deserve it.

This is why we see people defending celebrities' bad behavior when they go on racist tirades, film sex tapes, or get accused of heinous crimes—because it's just too hard a pill to swallow to accept that their beloved national treasure childhood hero could actually turn out to be not as much of a shining star as they thought. On a more personal level, the halo effect could mean making excuses for people and making relationship decisions based on how you want to see people or how you saw them initially, and not based on how they are portraying themselves to be right now. If when you initially met Bobby he was a saint, but a little later, he seems to have somehow gone from zero to douchebag in 3 weeks flat, don't be afraid to stop and reconsider the relationship.

One final type of cognitive bias that can affect decision making is survivorship bias. This one usually works against us particularly when it comes to life choices or risky ventures that we are considering. Survivorship bias runs on the consensus that we are more likely to remember a loud success, than we are to remember a quiet failure. So we are more likely to see a venture, career path, or investment as less risky if we hear of many loud successes.

A great example of this is in the world of MLM (that's "multi-level marketing"—less affectionately called "pyramid schemes"). MLM companies are masters at leveraging survivorship bias to get new people to join. Realistically, hundreds of thousands of people have failed at MLM–far more than have joined and succeeded. Yet, the ones who have joined and succeeded are very loud and proud about their success, and the ones who failed typically walk away quietly and try to pretend to forget that they ever even tried it in the first place.

MLMs love to bombard you with the stories of people who paid for their nephew's college tuition, bought their 6 bedroom house outright, and paid cash for their dad's heart transplant, all with the money they made recruiting people to their team of representatives, ambassadors, tribe members, or whatever other term the MLM comes up with to describe the people who join them. As a result of this survivorship bias, our evaluation is skewed.

Just because Johnny next door sells essential oils with his MLM and does well enough for you to grumble in envy every time you see his Lexus parked in his driveway, it doesn't mean you should go out and rush to quit your job and liquidate your emergency fund to put down that $3,000 to jump in on the essential oil game. And just because Michael Jordan became a great basketball player, it doesn't mean it's automatically easy for you to do that too. Survivorship bias does not just happen with MLM companies or the field of professional sports either. Although these are great examples, it happens in many different types of scenarios.

Virtually any situation that has a high risk and high reward associated with it has some form of survivorship bias weaved in, causing people to be less likely to have fears about the potential for failure and more likely to feel confident about the small potential for success. Now this is not all to dash your hopes and dreams and say that you should never strive towards any meaningful goals or success because it seems difficult or unlikely. But just make sure that when you're making choices, you're getting all the information so you can see things clearly and make the best and right choice for you. Don't let survivorship bias cloud your judgment.

Paradox Of Choice

Another reason why you suck at making choices is simply because you have way too damn many. As humans, for some reason, it's our nature to believe that the more options we have in front of us, the higher the chance that we are to be presented with the best possible option, and therefore, the more likely we are to end up with a favorable choice. There's a weird psychology that makes us skeptical of settling down with the first person we date, running with the first idea that pops into our heads, and picking the first appealing thing that stands out to us on the menu. We believe that if we have several options in front of us, it'll make it easier to pick the best one.

However, there is actually a psychological study that suggests that the exact opposite is, in fact, the truth when it comes to making decisions. In 1995, Sheena Iyengar, a business professor at Columbia University, conducted a very interesting experiment. She set up a sample booth of different jams at a California market. Every couple hours, she swapped the selection of jams between 24 choices, and 6 choices. More people were drawn to the sample booth when the larger variety of options was present, but regardless of the number of options present, whether presented with 24 or 6 jams, consumers on average only sampled two. And perhaps most interesting of all, *ten times* more people purchased after sampling from the small assortment than from the large assortment. Anyone else craving PB&J right now? Just me? Okay, moving on.

So what does that all tell us? That people are stupid and don't know a good thing when it's in front of them? Nah. It shows us that the more options you have available to you, the harder it is actually going to be for you to make a decision because of the additional possibilities you have to consider. What's also interesting about the paradox of choice is that the more options you have, the less likely you are to be happy with your ultimate decision.

It's quite screwed up if you think about it. For as much as we constantly complain about how we just want to be able to do what we want, we rarely know with certainty what it even is that we want to do. For as much as we constantly preach that we want to be happy, we rarely know with certainty what exactly it is that would make us so. What we think will make us happy, we attain, and then we're left confused as to why we are still not eternally smiling and laughing like a Tickle-Me-Elmo.

Forget about big life choices for a minute. Think about the simple task of going out to dinner. Does this sound familiar?

Guy: Where do you want to go for dinner?

Girl: I don't care. Anywhere is fine.

Guy: Alright, let's go to the Mexican place.

Girl: No, not Mexican.

Guy: Alright, how about Italian?

Girl: Nah...

This goes on over and over ad nauseum until you've named every single country in the world and eventually the couple either dies of hunger or breaks up.

These conversations seem to go a little better, though, when they go more like this:

Guy: Do you want Mexican or Italian for dinner?

Girl: Let's do Mexican. That sounds good.

See how much faster that was? Now you can be on your merry way, get to actually eat tonight, and as a bonus, you get to keep your relationship in tact. When having to pick from an endless supply of options, nothing comes to mind, and nothing sounds right. But if there's just a couple options, you're more likely to be pleased with your choice, and it's infinitely faster and easier to decide because you just have to pick one of them. You just have to come up with an answer to a multiple choice question, instead of also coming up with all the potential answers to the multiple choice question, and then picking the final answer on top of that. You know you loved those multiple choice tests in school. Picking one from three is a lot easier, quicker, and less mentally taxing than picking one from three million...or infinity.

So it's all about finding the balance. If you are not presented with enough choices—say you're only given one thing take it or leave it—you are going to feel restricted, and you are going to protest the option in front of you, even if it is one that you might typically be more than happy to choose. If *Guy* said "we're having Mexican tonight," *Girl* may not have gone for that even though she likes Mexican food. So if you have too many choices, your brain is going to get overwhelmed and either completely check out, resist locking in on one decision, or respond with something like "whatever." But a restricted number of choices makes it so that your brain will have an easier time deciding what it actually wants—which, as we've learned, is very important when it comes to food and restaurants.

When the paradox of choice is working against you, rather than lucking up on an epiphany about exactly what you want to eat and then ordering that, you instead find yourself standing in line at Baskin Robbins with your butt cheeks sweating as you wipe perspiration from your brow and grind your teeth, while trying to decide what you want and scaring the other onlooking customers in the process. And it never seems to get easier, either, as you begin to realize that you are an incredibly, shamefully indecisive person and now you're left feeling as though you need to ditch the idea of deciding altogether and go away for a while to mull it over.

In most cases, when it comes to the little things, when you leave the site of a decision, you make it more likely that you will never come back to finish the decision because there was simply way too much for you to try to sort through in your mind in the first place and it has left you feeling overly stressed. When you're asked what flavor ice cream you want, and your response is "I need to sleep on it" or "Can I use a lifeline?," you know you're in trouble and the paradox of choice is working against you.

Businesses actually recognize the power of this principle, and they take advantage of it by using it as a valuable tool when it comes to promoting sales. This is why when you go to high-end places, there are usually only a few options available for you to pick from. Going back to a restaurant example (Can you tell how much I love food?), if you go to a super bougie spot, you may have just three dinner options, or two set fixed courses of meals. Now, these options are likely going to cost you approximately the same as a small house in the Midwest, but at least the fact that you don't have many choices means that you are going to decide in minutes vs hours, and while you're spending more money on food, you get to save money on medical bills to treat what otherwise would have been a brain aneurism from option overload.

As much as I love to go eat at the Cheesecake Factory, their menu is basically a chapter book, and I can't help but feel like I'm on the hook for a book report after going through it. Sometimes the stress alone from the idea of going through their menu is enough to make me choose to eat elsewhere. Multinational Consumer Goods giant Procter & Gamble has seen the concept of the paradox of choice play out firsthand. They ironically found decreasing the number of varieties of their popular Head & Shoulders shampoo brand resulted in a 10% increase in sales.

So to summarize, having access to too many different choices is not going to make you happy. It is going to make you miserable, stressed, and confused, and make you miss out on going to one of your favorite restaurants. Instead of going places that have too many options or believing that infinity choices is going to make you happy, recognize that your brain is one totally screwed up, lazy organ that would actually prefer to just be told what to do, or at the very least what to choose from. The more narrowed down your options are, the better.

You Are Not Using Your Brain

Or, more specifically, you are not using your brain *effectively*. When it comes to making effective decisions, it's important to learn how to use your brain as a processor rather than a hard drive. You want to get into the habit of using it to make sense of information, not store it. Far too many people treat their brain like a hard drive and overload it with a ton of useless information and then expect it to work smoothly, and quickly find and process whatever is needed at the time. Just like a real hard drive (or your poor friend that everyone vents their problems to), the brain just ends up getting extremely bogged down and totally bummed out by the fact that you are asking way too much of it.

It cannot adequately review and process information when you're filling it to the brim first and then asking for it to serve you in any given way. I mean, to be fair, how well do you function when you're stuffed to the gills with turkey on Thanksgiving Day? The more you try to ask a full brain to make fast decisions, the harder it is going to be because now you're also exerting an intense amount of pressure on yourself that leaves you feeling overwhelmed and exhausted.

You need to learn how to process information effectively. A great strategy for this is to avoid taking in information in the first place. For a bigger decision, take all the information you know that could play a role in your ultimate choice, write it down on a piece of paper and begin processing through the information in front of you. Removing this information from your mind and placing it before you to be analyzed will help free up the mental space needed to really get into the decision-making process. Now, you're not asking your brain to facilitate too many functions at once. Although you may have a supercomputer between your ears, it can still be pretty archaic if you're not working together with your inner operating system to help it function to its highest ability.

CHAPTER 4

THE ROOT

LIKE ALL PROBLEMS, there is a root. And like all problems, people are mostly unaware of that root, and are therefore powerless to address it or remove it. There are many potential "roots" that can contribute to the reason why a person would be so indecisive. One of these roots may sound familiar and applicable to you, or perhaps many will. Next, to give you an idea of what areas you need to start to attack and fix, we are going to get into some of the fundamental primary issues that cause chaos in your decision-making process, contributing to indecisiveness.

Low Self-Confidence

Have you ever had to make a big decision and felt a twinge of fear in your stomach rise up because you were afraid of what other people might think about you and the decision that you would make? This could be something as small and common as deciding between wearing something that's a little more dressed up, sexy, or "out there" that's expressive of your personality and how you feel, or wearing a boring, modest little potato sack that you feel other people would be more approving of or comfortable with. Or it could be something bigger like deciding between living in LA or Idaho, or being a writer, or a podiatrist (*I'm talking to you, Dad*). Have you ever found yourself leaning more towards what another person wanted instead of what you want?

Low self-confidence is at the root of this, and it can be a huge knife in the back to the decision-making process for people who find themselves struggling to feel confident in their own desires. It is not uncommon for people to be raised believing that their own judgment or desires are "wrong" or "unimportant" and that someone else's judgment or desires are more valuable. In fact, many people are raised with this false notion and find themselves struggling to shake it, and therefore struggle to make decisions in adulthood as a result of it.

The thing with low self-confidence being a kick to the gonads when you are making decisions is that sometimes the "voice" that you are arguing with has nothing to do with your current reality at all. Sometimes, that voice that you are arguing with is someone in your head that you continue to think about even years later, like a mean aunt or a bully from school. You may continue to remember that one nasty thing they said to you about something or another and now every time you go to make a related decision, you hear that voice in your head and you begin to doubt yourself over it. If this is the case, then you need to up your game with your self-confidence so that you can tell that nasty imaginary voice in your head, or the judgmental people outside of you where they can shove it so that you can get back to making decisions for yourself rather than making decisions for everyone else around you.

When you build up this confidence, it becomes easier for you to start choosing in favor of what *you* want and tune out the irrelevant voices and noise of everyone else, unless you consciously and voluntarily deem that someone else's opinion genuinely does hold validation in a decision that you are preparing to make. You can up your self-confidence, when it comes to decision making specifically, by just making more decisions on your own without outside influence, starting with small things. Like I said earlier, every day, we make approximately *zillions* of decisions—what to wear, what to eat, what to say to that weird person who keeps staring at you, to hold your pee or go to the bathroom later.... all of these decisions have consequences or results, most non-fatal.

As you are making decisions over the course of the day, tune in to each choice you make, and don't get any input from anyone else. Make your own decision, review the outcome, realize that everything worked out and nobody died, and rinse and repeat, being sure to especially praise yourself along the way for decisions that turn out exceptionally well. This will over time build your confidence in your own decision making, from the little things, all the way up to the big things, so when someone asks you "paper or plastic?", you won't have to turn to the guy in line behind you to help you decide.

The Stranger In The Mirror

Some people struggle to make decisions because when it comes to knowing themselves....they don't. If you are someone who has struggled to make decisions because it is hard for you to determine what is right *for you,* the root cause of this may just be a low level of self-knowledge that leaves you unsure about what on earth you like, want, or value. Think about it: if you do not know what your favorite color is and someone asks you, what are you going to say? How are you going to feel? Likely, you will find that you are feeling overwhelmed and unsure and you may make a guess or spit out something random, but in reality, you have no idea because you just don't know who you are and what you like. So when it comes time to make more important choices in your life than telling someone your favorite color, you are struggling to make a decision because somehow, even after multiple decades of living in your body, you still do not have one damn clue as to who you are and what you want from this life.

In some cases, you are going to be faced with decisions that you don't know how to make because you have never had to explore this part of yourself in the past or you've never faced a similar situation. For example, if someone asks if you want a bubble tea with almond milk or a bubble tea with oat milk, you may have no idea how to respond because you have never had either of these before and therefore you have no idea as to how they taste or whether or not you actually like them. In this situation, it is natural that you would not know how to respond because you simply have not experienced either.

But there are other situations where even if you have not experienced any of the options before you, if you know yourself, you would still know how to choose. If you were deciding between two colleges, or two career paths, you should know yourself enough to know which one to choose based on which one aligns most with your likes, dislikes, strengths, goals, values, etc. So it is essential that you really get to know who you are and spend a little more time asking yourself the important questions, so you'll hopefully be able to spend a little less time wiping the sweat off your brow.

The F-Word

Fear. As we discussed previously, one big reason why people struggle to make decisions is because they are afraid. They're shaking in their boots, scared to death of making the wrong decision and suffering from the consequences that would theoretically follow. In bigger situations, the fear of making a wrong choice is totally valid and is a perfectly good reason for someone to need to slow down and be cautious about making their final choice to ensure that they avoid dealing with unnecessary consequences.

If you're in a relationship with someone whom you love, but lately, you have been arguing a lot, you may be wrestling with deciding as to whether or not it is even worth it for the two of you to stay together. This is a toughie. On the one hand, you risk staying in a relationship that is filled with friction and arguments that may not get better, while on the other hand, you risk leaving behind someone that you love. Both of these seem risky and can have negative or painful consequences, making it challenging for you to really make a decision and commit to it. In a situation like this, butt-clenching fear is totally expected because either way you are facing some pretty tall challenges.

Oftentimes, however, fear from very valid life situations like the one above can begin to trickle over into smaller decisions. For example, you may have a fear of deciding between two different vacation locations because you are afraid that you are going to be disappointed with the choice that you pick. Maybe you worry that you will wish you had gone to the other location because the climate would have been better, or your accommodations would have been nicer, or your Instagram pics would have turned out more envy-worthy, or simply because you are afraid over something that you are not even really sure of.

Yes, I'm talking about FOMO—the fear of missing out. And it is a very real and totally overwhelming fear that many people face on a regular basis. If you are finding that you have constant concern over making the wrong choice or of having unwanted consequences from the choice that you make, there is a good chance that your indecision stems from fear itself.

Analysis Paralysis

Analysis paralysis ties in with the paradox of choice. Analysis paralysis happens when there are too many options available or when you have put way more pressure on a decision than you need to, so you find yourself struggling to commit one way or the other. When you are dealing with analysis paralysis, you will know because it is always accompanied by an extreme feeling of overwhelm and the inability to move forward. You will feel paralyzed from your over-thinking. Analysis paralysis often comes with a fairly high degree of fear because the individual that is struggling to make the decision is afraid that they are going to make the wrong one, which is generally why they overwhelm themselves with the facts. As you know, attempting to take on all of that information only results in your brain getting overloaded and struggling with the decision-making process even more.

Analysis paralysis is quite common in scenarios where you have to make a rather big decision, especially when you are not used to making decisions of that nature or magnitude. As a simple example, if you are making the decision to invest $5,000 into the stock market, you may find yourself overwhelmed because given the uncertain outcome, you are unsure as to whether or not you want to risk that money. You may begin to over analyze the pros and cons of both choices as an effort to see which is going to be the most responsible one, only to find yourself feeling totally unconfident in either decision.

In these situations, it can be helpful to ensure that you are not putting too much pressure on yourself and are taking adequate time to process the information, then choosing one, and committing to your choice and giving it a chance to work out. Sometimes, there is no clear right or wrong answer, since (aside from the wonderous Magic 8 Ball) we don't have an ability to predict the future. You just need to make an evaluation with all the information you have at the time, then square up your shoulders and go forward with confidence.

Apathy

Sometimes, you just don't give a shit. And not caring enough about an outcome can be just as problematic as caring too much about an outcome. Apathy is actually a big reason for indecisiveness, and at times it can also become highly problematic...especially when it comes to relationships where we want the other person to care about something as much as we do. If you're stoked about movie night and you've been looking forward to it all week to the point that you've been looking up gourmet popcorn recipes on Pinterest, and you ask your boyfriend if he prefers to watch *The Notebook* or *Sleepless in Seattle*, chances are his eyes are going to glaze over because he genuinely does not care.

To him, both may be totally uninteresting, and he is really only there watching them because he wants to hang out with you. When situations like this come up in relationships, people can tend to take it personally because they view the person's disinterest in the situation as a disinterest in them. Of course, it would feel way better for you if they showed the same interest in "your thing" as you and took a part in making related decisions around it, but let's be real here: if they don't care, they just don't care.

If you are only experiencing apathy in situations that genuinely mean nothing to you, then apathy is generally not a problem, and you can easily just chalk it up to that.

If, however, you find yourself constantly apathetic towards everything and you are having a hard time caring about any decisions that need to be made, you may want to talk to a doctor. Just giving it to you real, this can be a sign of depression or something similar, and having someone to talk to who can offer you genuine support may be what you need to overcome this challenge as well as some others that you may be facing, too.

Unnecessary Caretaking

While people may assume that women are more apt to be the victims in this kind of situation, this is a genderless issue. A fair number of people find themselves facing the challenge of being on the wrong side of a relationship that involves unnecessary caretaking. If you are one of them, you will know because you will be struggling to make decisions for fear of hurting someone else. Now, we're not talking here about necessary caretaking—we're talking about the kind of caretaking that always results in one person always sacrificing themselves and getting the short end of the stick because they're overly concerning themselves with looking after someone else who is often oblivious to the gravity of the burden being taken on by the other person. We're talking about one person overly concerning themselves with another person's decisions, outcomes, or life to the point of being willing to lose themselves and absorb the other person's consequences. This is ultimately a sign of a codependent relationship.

Unnecessary caretaking and low self-confidence can often go hand-in-hand, but if you examine each of these issues separately, the specific problems that you are facing are totally different. With low self-confidence, you are worrying about what other people will think of you or say to you. With unnecessary care-taking, you are worrying about how your choices will affect the wellbeing of other people. To a degree, this is an important thing to think about. After all, you don't want to go through life as a pompous my-way-or-the-highway self-absorbed douche who only thinks about themselves, not giving a crap about how anyone else feels and as a result repeatedly makes decisions that lead to negative consequences for people around you. However, you also do not want to be giving up on your own desires at best in lighter situations, or your own wellbeing at worst in more serious situations.

For instance, let's say you have a BFF who you know is not a big fan of pineapples on pizza but to you, Hawaiian pizza is God's gift to mankind. Right now, there just so happens to be a special on your favorite pizza and you and your friend are deciding between paying more for their fave or paying less for your fave. Are you going to go ahead and pay more for the pepperoni that you do not really like because your friend prefers it, or are you going to save money and get the pizza that you like? Who's going to be the one to pick the toppings off?

If you're thinking go along with your friend's pick, you may think that you are just being humble and nice and generous. And if you are only making decisions this way every once in a while, then chances are that yes, you are simply being generous and thoughtful. However, if you are constantly choosing what someone else would want because you want them to be happy, even when it comes to insignificant little things like pepperoni on pizza, and you are never happy with the outcome, you need to make a change. Bear with me on the example—if you're one of those people who loves to find holes in everything, you're probably thinking *"these people are both idiots, everyone just buy your own damn pizza and get what you want, problem solved."* If you're thinking this...yes, you're right. But you're missing the point.

The point is, there is nothing "nice" or "thoughtful" about constantly valuing other people more than yourself, as this only leads to resentment and negative cycles in your relationships. If one person is always giving in and sacrificing in a relationship, things need to change. You shouldn't always be the one who has to pick off the toppings. And conversely, while we're on the subject, you shouldn't always be the one who forces everyone else to pick off the toppings.

CHAPTER 5

HOW BIG ARE YOUR POTATOES?

BACK IN THE 1800S, when potato farmers were selling their produce, the small potatoes didn't make them as much money as the larger ones. They weren't making them as much money as they could be, but they provided enough money to get by until the bigger potatoes came in. The small potatoes were basically insignificant and didn't have the level of positive returns that the big ones did. So over time, the phrase "small potatoes" essentially came to mean that something was insignificant, meaningless, or unimportant.

No, you're not a potato farmer in the 1800s, but you do have potatoes. You have "small potatoes"—decisions that are relatively insignificant or unimportant, and you have the occasional "big potatoes"—decisions that actually are significant and important. And being able to effectively gauge the importance of your decision and what will come of it is an important way for you to be able to start working through your decision-making process at reasonable speeds. Being able to decipher between a small and a large decision means that you can take some of the pressure off when it makes sense. Alleviating the pressure on yourself on the little things will give you more energy for the big things. All potatoes are not created equal. And all decisions are not created equal. Are you sweating over small potatoes, or big ones?

And it's not just the decisions themselves that come in the form of small or large potatoes. Decision-making criteria can also range from tall to venti. When it comes to making choices, humans, in general, have a tendency to fixate on all the unimportant information and ignore the info that actually matters. When you buy a car, are you more focused on its reputation for reliability and its crash test results? Or are you more concerned with whether the color scheme of the car fits the color scheme of your Instagram page? That beautiful black convertible with the red leather interior is going to fall apart before you can even finish your first year's payments—something you would know if you made your car buying decision based on things that actually mattered. Our logic can be very twisted and broken when we are making decisions, which can lead to us making choices that later lead to serious regrets which, as you can imagine, makes future decisions even scarier.

It's Probably Not That Deep

As you have already learned, not every decision is super deep, therefore not every decision needs you to handle it with as much grace as the Queen of England handles her wave. Although you already have the awareness to understand that not all decisions are deep, you may not yet have the understanding of how you can relieve some of the pressure off of yourself for decisions that truly do not matter so much.

Start by looking at your decision and getting ridiculously clear with yourself on how that decision impacts you and what it is impacting overall. Ask yourself questions like "How will this impact me in one week? Six weeks? Six months? Six years?" Chances are, most of your decisions are not actually going to impact you in the long run so there is no reason as to why you should have to put so much pressure on every single choice as if it were deciding which wire to snip to dismantle an atomic bomb. Instead, take things for what they are and start putting the pressure on them accordingly. If the worst thing that is going to happen is you don't like the taste of your meal or you'll wish you had worn a different shirt later that day, then you can count yourself pretty lucky since neither of these is that meaningful. If, however, the worst thing that is going to happen is that you are going to lose your home, go broke, lose your partner, or end up severely ill or injured, then maybe you should take that decision a little more seriously.

At the end of the day, I suppose every decision *could* impact the outcome of your life down the line, but could you imagine how exhausting that would be to have to think *everything* through in this way? Could you imagine if every time you left your house to go for a walk, you thought "Well, I could turn right, but they're doing roadwork over there, and I could fall into a manhole and drown in sewage or turn into a teenage mutant ninja turtle. Or, I could turn left, but there's a piano store that way and someone could be having a piano delivered, and as they're loading it onto the delivery truck, it could roll out into the street and run me over, crushing my legs and my life dream of running a marathon. I mean I guess technically, that *could* happen. Or, you know, more likely, it would totally not. You can't predict the future five decades down the line and you can't control every variable and possible outcome, and living as if you can is way too exhausting and absolutely not worth it.

Small Potatoes In A Flash

Once you have effectively gauged the size of the potatoes in your garden, you can go ahead and start managing them depending on their size. For smaller potatoes, you want to handle them quickly and in a flash. Deep fry those bad boys. Anything that will not affect you in the long run or result in serious injury or death is a small potato. These decisions may have an impact on your day, but they're not going to ruin your life.

Give yourself a time limit for these decisions. And make it brief. Ever heard of Parkinson's Law? The more time we think we have to do something, the more time we take to do it. You think you have four and a half weeks to make a PowerPoint? Guess what? It's going to take you four and a half weeks to make it. Think you have four and a half days to make that PowerPoint? Somehow, you're going to magically find a way to do it in four and a half days.

Most small potatoes don't need any more than five to ten seconds to decide. So put the mental timer on, and think fast. Be observant and take inventory of the result of the decision. If it turns out well, you'll have positive feedback, knowing that everything worked out okay. If it turns out not so well, take note of how you could make a better decision next time. Eventually, you'll find that picking gets easier and faster, and the decision anxiety diminishes.

A Recipe For Big Potatoes

When you do find that you are dealing with something that is actually worth the time of day, you are going to need to learn how to slow down and actually make these decisions properly. Big potatoes are anything that is likely to impact you long-term, and the longer it will impact you, the bigger that potato is. Car loans, mortgages, marriages, career changes, moving to a new state, quitting your job to become an alpaca farmer, breeding...these are our big potatoes, as they have the most potential impact long term.

So what do we do with big potatoes? We're not going to flash fry them. We're going to pull out the slow-cooker for these. But note, that slow cooker does still have a timer. Parkinson's Law is always at work. So even for big decisions, you still need a time limit because you can't take forever to make any choice, whether large or small—eventually, you have to decide and move forward.

The first thing you want to do is slow down. You don't

want to slow down to the point of hiding under a rock for ten years, but you do want to slow down enough to actually consider the impact and possible outcomes from all angles to make sure that you are making the decision intentionally.

Then, accept it. Just accept that this is not a quickie. It's going to take you a little bit of time to evaluate this one. It's like hitting a traffic jam when you're on your way somewhere. Yes, you want to get there faster, but it does you no benefit to rush and freak out when you're in complete gridlock. You don't get there faster. You just get there angrier.

The next thing you have to do is be ridiculously honest with yourself and then commit to staying in integrity with who you are. Remember, big decisions are going to impact you for a long time, so you will not benefit from letting someone else make these decisions for you or weigh in their opinion to the point that you stop caring about yours. While there will be times where someone else's input will be valuable, at the end of the day, what affects your life is up to you, and you're the one that has to live with it.

What lifestyle do you want to live, and what decision is going to help you live that lifestyle? What other areas of your life will be affected? If it is a decision about moving and where you want to relocate to, it's also going to impact your career, your friendships, your finances, your day to day lifestyle, your income, and your happiness. So look at the big picture.

When it comes to these bigger decisions, don't be afraid to

even schedule out some time for you to think about it. Unlike with small potatoes, with bigger potatoes, you don't want to rush. One way that many people fail themselves in big decisions is by not giving themselves adequate time to clearly think about what it is that they want. Another issue with bigger decisions is constantly mulling over them. People may find themselves consumed by this decision in everything they do. Every time they have a moment of free time, and every moment that they're engaged in doing something else, they're consumed by this pending decision, causing mounting fear and anxiety.

So don't let it consume your every waking moment and your entire life. Set aside a set time to examine the pros and cons, and figure out what you want to do about that choice. And any other time outside of that window, don't allow yourself to think about it. Don't amplify your stress leading up to it. Teach yourself to wait until the scheduled time. And in order to really make the most out of this scheduled time, make sure that you release any attachment to thoughts about the decision before your scheduled time arises. Then, after the scheduled time has passed, mentally walk away. Refrain from holding on to the process and going over it again and again to make sure that you have made the right decision. Trust that you made the right choice, and use this as an opportunity to grow your self-confidence in your skills and in your ability to see things through and generate a positive outcome as a result.

You need to be willing to stay committed to your decision long enough to see if it works or not. Committing to an exercise plan for one meal is not going to do you any good. Moving to another city, and moving back before you can even unpack because you get homesick your first night isn't helping you either. You're in control. You reserve the right to change your mind, but don't do it too soon before you even have all the facts of the outcome.

Lastly, you can always reach out for support in making your decision if you are having an especially hard time. The key here is ensuring that you are only receiving support and that no one is deciding for you. You are an adult, so letting Mommy and Daddy decide the outcome of your life is not a good idea. And allowing people to weigh in their opinion and help expand your perception and see things you're not seeing is only helpful when it's people who know you well, and potentially people who have a life or outcome similar to the one you want. So don't just let any and everybody say their piece. Not all outside opinions are to be weighed equally.

Potato Chopping

Did you know that there are people who eat planes? If you're reading, no, that's not a typo. If you're listening, no, you're not hearing things. No, you didn't accidentally switch to a different audiobook. Yes, this may seem totally random, but it's surprisingly relevant to what I'm about to say. So as I was saying, there are people—human people like you and me—who eat planes—like *make sure your seat backs and tray tables are in their full upright position* planes. French entertainer Michel Lotito went down in history in 1980 as a man who ate an entire airplane—a

Cessna 150 to be exact, from nose to tail, and everything in between. He also ate 6 chandeliers, 7 TVs, 2 beds, 18 bicycles, and a coffin.

I mention this not because I recommend it, but because of the way that he did it—one piece at a time. The idea is to take one seemingly impossibly overwhelmingly huge thing and make it feel easy and doable by breaking it down into smaller pieces. Treat your bigger decisions like this. If a decisions feels too big, it could be because that one decision actually involves many. Break them down into smaller decisions that are quicker and easier to make. Got big potatoes? Dice those puppies. Make the big easier by making it small.

Sometimes, breaking down these larger and more challenging decisions into ones that are smaller and broken up makes it easier for you to commit to a decision right from the start because you are no longer trying to decide everything all at once. The pressure of the situation is taken off, and you have an easier time making decisions because you are no longer trying to decide everything all in one go a hundred steps down the line. You just commit to the first step and move on with your life.

CHAPTER 6

ALRIGHT? ALRIGHT.

HAVE you ever answered a question with a question to receive more information about the original question, thus allowing you to decide what your answer to the original question ought to be? Have you ever heard a question where the word "question" was used so many times? In the last chapter, we talked about figuring out what decisions are important and which are not, and how to make decisions around those decisions accordingly. Sometimes, coming to a conclusion about what to do requires gathering more information. And that requires asking questions. Asking questions about questions can be a great way for you to gather the information that you need in order to feel confident about the choice that you are making. Sometimes, the questions that you ask are going to be just for you. Other times, in tougher situations, the questions may need to be directed towards someone else you trust for help or someone who may have more information or experience than you.

At the end of the day, you are the only one who is really going to know what it is that you need to be asking yourself to get to the answers that you need to get to in order for you to make a decision. So this is not by any means a comprehensive list. However, there are some standard questions that you can ask to help you start sorting through the mess of confusion in your brain, thus helping you get to the answer that you are looking for. You can add or also take away from these lists as you see fit. Typically, the questions you ask are going to vary depending on whether you are trying to answer something that is quick and insignificant, or something that is more long term and more significant. So for decisions, big and small, here's a little cheat sheet of questions you can ask yourself so you have them all in one place.

Questions For Small Potatoes

Sometimes you don't need questions for these at all. But sometimes you do. If you are looking to find an answer quickly or to something not particularly important, such as if your friend is waiting on you for an answer as to if you're down for getting together this weekend, or if a waitress is waiting for you to order, you're not going to want nor need to sit there asking yourself a zillion questions. I mean, nobody wants to sit and wait around for you indefinitely. They might be smiling on the outside, but both the waitress and your dinner date are mentally stabbing you in the leg with your dinner fork.

So here are three quick questions for those quick decisions:

1. Will this decision make me happy?
2. If not, why not, and can I make a different decision instead?
3. Am I capable of fulfilling the obligation? (Can I afford what I'm considering purchasing, do I have time to devote to the task I'm agreeing to take on? Etc.)

After answering these three questions, you should feel confident that you have the information that you need to make the decision that is going to be right for you. If you still feel stumped afterward, give your head a shake because you probably failed to actually answer the questions in the first place and you're probably mistaking small potatoes for big ones.

Questions For Big Potatoes

Small potato questions can typically be asked from memory, where even necessary at all. But when it comes to larger decisions, sometimes, it is not quite so easy, and you're going to need to put in a little more leg work to get to the answer that is right for you. So in addition to asking deeper questions, you might want to actually write things down. If you are wanting to decide on whether or not to buy a house, to select a business partner, or to move to a foreign country, you'll need to not only ask deeper questions, but you'll also need to ask more questions, so you can make sure you are uncovering enough information to make it so you don't feel like you screwed yourself in the end. Make sure you are answering honestly and objectively. Don't overinflate the answers to these questions just because it's a bigger decision.

Here's a list of questions to get you started:

1. What is at stake here?
2. What is the potential long term impact of this decision?
3. What is the worst that could happen?
4. How and how quickly could I recover if the worst case scenario did happen?
5. If I don't do this now, am I going to regret that?
6. What am I so afraid of?
7. What do I really want?
8. What am I doing this for?
9. Who am I doing this for?
10. Can I respect myself after making this decision?
11. Will I like myself after making this decision?

Answering these questions is of course going to help you learn more about the situation itself, but it will also help you learn more about yourself—knowledge that can make future decisions easier. By answering these questions, you will find out if the decision you are considering is something that is going to help you advance in your life in a positive direction, or if it is something that you will regret or that will hold you back. Knowing these answers will make you feel confident not only making the decision, but also sticking to it.

Make sure you are in the right state of mind when going through these questions. And make sure you have all the facts. Avoid making decisions when you are not fully clear on what all your options are, or what all they entail. You don't want to get stuck signing a check that you can't cash. There's a reason why they say don't sign contracts until you have read the fine print. While not every decision you make is going to have any level of legal obligation involved, decisions do frequently come with details that you may have wished you had access to beforehand so that you were not left in the dark and disappointed with the outcome in the end. Before you agree to anything, always be very clear about what it is that you are agreeing to so that you can stand fully behind that agreement if that is what you desire to do. Otherwise, do not agree.

CHAPTER 7
THE EASY BUTTON

WE KNOW that potatoes come both big and small, and we're now armed with some key questions we can use to handle each. But the problem is: sometimes, we don't have the mental energy to even handle the big potatoes because we're too hung up on the little guys. What do we need here? The Easy Button. There is a very powerful, very *easy* way that you can slap an "easy button" on your life and make those smaller decisions virtually effortless so that you have plenty of mental space to make those larger decisions you have been pondering. The best way to eliminate decision fatigue is to take advantage of the power of habits, and turn your habits into processes that serve your overall success.

Rather than getting into the habit of being indecisive about what you want to do each day, you can make habits so that you automatically do the things that you need to get done with ease and without thought or stress. Habits make our lives so much easier because our brains essentially go on autopilot when we start engaging in things we are already accustomed to doing over and over again. As a result, engaging in a habitual action takes significantly less mental energy than engaging in a non habitual action. When you're doing something that's a habit, you're doing something that your brain doesn't have to think through or figure out, meaning that there are virtually no decisions to be made. Sounds awesome, right?

For just a minute, I want you to see your brain like a machine that can be used to totally change your life because, truly, it is. Your brain operates just like a computer in that you can set up triggers that result in you having automatic processes or practices that can help you fulfill certain goals. On a computer, habits are equivalent to what is known as IFTT technology, or "if this then that" technology. This essentially means that if a trigger is pulled, such as if your computer is turned on, a certain process will launch, such as your desktop turning on and certain applications opening up. The cool thing is your brain can do exactly the same thing, where experiencing a trigger can create a certain behavioral response to that trigger.

This isn't news to you, though. You already deal with triggers on a daily basis. For example, when your alarm goes off in the morning, you wake up and immediately go brush your teeth. When your phone dings at you, you look at it. When you were a kid, you'd hear the garage door open up, and you'd scramble to your bedroom and throw everything in your closet so it looks like you cleaned your room like your parents told you to. These triggers exist everywhere in your daily life, although it is likely that you did not consciously create them, nor did you consciously create the routines that follow them.

Fortunately for you, these triggers are not exclusively ones that are pulled through unconscious behaviors, as you can actually create intentional triggers and intentional responses that allow you to have far more productive routines. If you don't feel the need to start completely anew, you can even create a new response to an existing trigger if you do not like the way that you are responding to said trigger. You just have to be willing to consciously identify that trigger and consciously recreate the response.

Creating your own triggers and responses kills your need to make decisions because everything is already decided for you. Rather than having to decide what you are going to do and what order you are going to do it in, you have already consciously made the decisions and ordered everything in an optimal manner so that you are able to simply go through the motions. This way, you are not wasting any brain power on having to consciously decide what to do next, which way to do it, and what needs to get done when because you have already set up the routine.

Create Decision-Serving Habits

Habits are specific ways that we tend to do specific things. My handy dandy dictionary says that a habit is "a settled or regular tendency or practice, especially one that is hard to give up." When we think about habits, sometimes we first think about bad or unwanted ones. An example of an unwanted habit is smoking to the detriment of your lungs or drinking copious amounts of coffee to the point where you're losing sleep and your heartrate can barely keep up. These types of habits are often addictions because people who engage in them have a hard time stopping, and find themselves feeling completely incapable of making new, healthier decisions. Of course, these habits can be broken, but depending on the nature of the habit, they can be especially difficult to break if chemical and psychological dependency and withdrawal symptoms are involved.

Habits are not all bad though. They are actually quite positive if we use them to our benefit, such as having the habit of choosing healthy foods off the menu, having the habit of setting a budget at the beginning of each month, or having the habit of showing your partner you love them on a daily basis.

Creating new habits for yourself ultimately starts with you determining where you can improve in your life and what habits or behaviors could help you improve in that way. If it's better health you're after, eating healthier, exercising more, and drinking more water are great places to start. Over time (at least 21 days seems to be the common consensus), the consistency of you engaging in these behaviors eventually turns them into a habit, which makes them become more automatic and less of a mental burden. You'll no longer have to think about it as much or talk yourself out of and into and out of it again because your brain has formed a new neural pathway that makes this habit automatic.

The key to actually forming these habits is to have triggers that stimulate them. If you think about it, virtually everything we do is stimulated by a trigger. Unfortunately, that trigger happens to often be stress or fear, two of our most influential triggers in our unconscious minds. You can use stress and fear to trigger your new habits, or you can choose new triggers to help you begin engaging in new and positive habits.

If it's a goal of yours to drink less soda and drink more water, instead of putting yourself in the position of having to choose what drink you want every time you end up at the checkout line, you can choose a trigger, then have your action as a result of the trigger be the one you want. Maybe you decide that every time you hear a car horn, you drink a cup of water. After purposefully doing this multiple times, the trigger and habit will both become automatic behaviors for you. Then, you'll get so accustomed to drinking water and will feel so satisfied from it, that you won't even want soda as much anymore. Then, you won't be in a position where you have to stress over making the right decision. With the right habits, certain decisions will be made for you. So find ways where you can form new habits to help you eliminate points of decision throughout your day. In doing so, you can make certain decisions either extinct or at the very least automatic by creating habits around them.

Create Routines For Yourself

A routine, according to the dictionary, is "a sequence of actions regularly followed; a fixed program." When you engage in a routine in your life, you are engaging in many different things in a specific order, using the same process every single time. You can think of a routine as kind of a series of habits. This could be your morning routine, the routine that you follow when you first arrive at work, or any other routine you engage in throughout your day or evening. Most of us unknowingly have developed routines based on what felt right at the moment, but have never stopped to consider whether or not our routines are still productive, positive, or if they even still fit our needs anymore. In most circumstances, they actually don't fit our needs anymore. We outgrow routines all the time, yet still engage in them because they have become so automatic to us. It is important to always be challenging our routines to see if it would behoove us to replace them or create new ones.

Creating routines for yourself starts with you deciding what needs to be done on a regular basis in your life. This should include the basic necessities and tasks and also actions that are in alignment with any future goals you have for yourself. Chances are you already have routines in place, so rather than creating routines, you need to optimize the ones that you already have. The best way for you to start optimizing your routines is to sit down and brainstorm every single routine that you presently have so that you can get a feel for what you are already doing and whether or not it is serving you. Write down every routine from how you wake up and get your day started, to how you manage your personal hygiene, how you start your work when you arrive at the office, or how you get your work done during the day.

You want to think of every single routine that you have, whether it is a daily, weekly, monthly, or yearly routine, and write it out in as much detail as possible, even down to the things you don't think matter. Seeing it all out on paper will help you visually see what needs to be eliminated or changed. Make sure you take your time, as you may find yourself forgetting steps since they have become so automatic to the point where you no longer even think about what it is that you are doing.

Once you have brainstormed all of your routines, you need to start asking yourself if they are actually serving you in getting everything you need done. The morning routine is a good place to start, as what happens in the morning sets the tone for the entire day. Having a good night routine is also helpful for bookending your day. That's a good time for you to get everything in order for your day tomorrow, so you're not spending precious time trying to decide between the blue shirt or the green shirt, the white socks or the gray socks, the Lucky Charms or the Cinnamon Toast Crunch. Choose your outfit in advance, set out your workout clothes, pack your laptop bag for work, and plan your breakfast. This will make your tomorrow run smoother, and you won't waste mental energy making menial decisions that keep you from having the clarity to make more important ones.

Lastly, once you've examined and recreated your routines, you should consider whether or not they are bringing happiness and joy to your life, as there is truly no point in engaging in lengthy routines if you are feeling drained or annoyed afterwards. If after you do your morning routine, you want to strangle someone, light something on fire, and then get back into bed, maybe you need to go back to the drawing board and rethink a few things. In most cases, you can balance your routines so that they include enjoyable practices and useful practices. You can work out in the morning and get a delicious protein shake after. You can tidy up your place while listening to your favorite playlist.

Keeping your routine joyful and fulfilling can help you enjoy life more in general, which will give your mental and emotional health a boost. So remember, if it's not fun *and* useful *to you*, that's not the routine for you. You want to create routines that you can enjoy and do long term. There's really no need of setting a routine of waking up at 3am, doing a dozen sun salutations, running 9 miles before the sun comes up to pick fresh produce from a nearby farm to make a green smoothie that tastes like butt if you absolutely hate it and can only muster up the strength to do it once in your lifetime.

Like a habit, the magic of a routine comes from repetition. It's not about proving what extraordinary string of events you can do once. It's about creating strings of events that fit both your goals and your lifestyle. Your routines should serve you, not serve to impress the people around you. Once you have identified where you can optimize your routines, you can rewrite them so that you know exactly how you want to do them going forward.

You, Incorporated

According to the Bureau of Labor Statistics, 50% of small businesses fail before they reach their fifth anniversary. Why do you think that is? How could that be? Why does such a high number of small businesses fail and fizzle out, yet big businesses seem to just get bigger? Because the man is trying to keep the little guy down so he stomps out anyone who has the nerve to shoot for an ounce of success just so he can laugh maniacally? No—the man has systems, templates, and processes. In doing this, they can create streamlined operations that take out all the extra thinking, figuring, and guesswork that go along with running a business. For the average small business, when they come to a task, each time is like they are doing it for the first time, even if it is a recurring task in their business. There are no scripts for sales calls, no templates for outreach emails, and no processes for getting customer reviews.

So every time they come to have to do a task, they have countless micro decisions they have to make in order to accomplish that task. Not only does this make things take forever and add unnecessary stress and confusion, it also results in inconsistencies, which makes it very difficult to reach goals and success metrics. So let that firmly imprint in that little noggin of yours how important establishing habits and routines is for your own life. You can think of habits as your systems and routines as your processes. The most successful and effective businesses have systems and processes. And the most successful and effective people have habits and routines.

You know another edge a franchise or a big business has over a struggling small business? Principles. Principles guide the direction of a business based on the most important goal, mission, and vision of that business. For example, a principle in a business could be to do what's best for the customer. Let's say you have a store. Right after ringing up a sale, the customer gets right at the exit and then drops the merch, smashing it into pieces. Then they come marching right back to you and demand a replacement. Butterfingers Brenda knows good and well that she broke the product when she let it slip out of her hands, and you know good and well that she doesn't deserve a replacement and you'd really rather give her a fist to the face instead. But if you abide by your principle to do what's best for the customer, you can instantaneously make the choice on how to move forward —the knuckle sandwich. Just kidding, you'd give her the replacement. So you don't have to decide what to do because the decision is already made for you. By having certain principles in place, businesses don't waste time making decisions or doubting them. You can do the same thing for yourself.

Come up with your own set of principles that can help you eliminate the need to make so many decisions. A principle could be as simple as *make your momma proud*, or *choose long term gratification over instant gratification*. If you have kids, it could be to do what's best for the kid. Ok, sure, every parent wants to do what's best for their kid. But if they actually keep that in mind, it can help them make better, quicker choices. So if it comes down to you choosing a job that pays 10% more, but forces you to work 50% more hours, choose what's best for the kid. If it comes down to choosing between two schools—one that's a little further away and costs more, or a much worse school that's closer and cheaper—do what's best for the kid.

If you don't have kids, and your principle is to choose long term gratification over instant gratification, when it comes time to pick between the salad or the fries, or working out or letting Netflix roll into the seventh episode in a row of *Big Bang Theory*, think long term gratification over instant gratification. Now, at the snap of your fingers, you've made your decision. No pros and cons lists, no phone a friend. Principles allow you to immediately make decisions instead of mulling them over endlessly.

Here's your homework: think of the different types of decisions you make on a regular basis, and come up with a brief list of overarching principles that you can use to help you make those decisions. Don't make it too lengthy. No need to make your own personal constitution. If you have to remember an entire Bible's worth of principles, well— you're just not going to. And if you can't remember your principles, how can they help you? They can't. So, keeping in mind your personal goals and the types of decisions you often have to make on a daily basis, create some principles, then pick the top few that can serve you best in the most situations. But most importantly, keep in mind that these principles need to be based on your values because they are essentially trump cards. So know what is most important to you first, then make your principles.

Become A Self-Imposed Snooze Fest

There's a reason why some of the world's most successful people are...well, in some ways downright boring. Sure, wearing a pink mohawk one day and then deciding to rock purple braids the next can feel like a satisfying statement of your individuality. Can you imagine someone like Steve Jobs with a pink mohawk? Well, if he did rock a pink mohawk, you can bet you'd have seen it every single day, because he knew the power of routine and repetition.

One of his trademarks was his cartoon character like wardrobe—in the sense that just like a cartoon character, Jobs wore the same thing every day. Jobs purchased a few of the same outfits and was famous for wearing those outfits everywhere he went, every single day. He owned a pair of blue jeans, a black turtleneck, and a pair of New Balance sneakers. And he was always seen in this exact same ensemble. Regular day at work? Black turtleneck. Important day at work? Black turtleneck. No work today? Black turtleneck.

When asked why he dressed like this, he said it was because it was one less decision he had to make each day, which kept him that much more involved in and better available for the more important decisions that needed to be made. He knew the importance of combatting decision fatigue. He knew that as the day goes on and the more decisions we make, the more our mental energy depletes, leaving our minds susceptible to making poorer choices. He didn't have brain cells to waste on what to wear—he had a multi-billion dollar company to run. And while you may not have a multi-billion dollar company to run, you probably do have at least one other thing on your to do list that's more important than picking out a t-shirt. And heck, maybe you would have a multi-billion dollar company to run if you didn't spend half the day in thinking man pose in your closet.

The mental clarity that Steve Jobs gained from eliminating insignificant decisions made him far more focused, decisive, productive, and ultimately profitable. And you can do the same for yourself. While you may not want to be totally boring and own one single outfit, you may want to take a page out of Jobs' book in certain areas of your life. The least you can do is put together your own outfits the night before so that each morning when you wake up, that's one less decision that you need to make in the morning.

Or, you can make routines around your crazy. Plan your individuality in advance. Choose a weekly routine for creativity of personal expression. You could have Mohawk Mondays and Whatever You Want Wednesdays. Assign a hairstyle or an outfit for each day, and then just leave one day of the week where you can let inspiration strike and do whatever the mood calls for. Obviously, you can (and should) do this for anything, not just your hair and outfits. It could be done for anything that you routinely have to make a decision on during the day. Here's another idea. Make a workout schedule in advance. Have a written plan of exactly how many reps of which exercises in which order, at which weights, using which equipment that you're going to do when you get to the gym. Not a fan of mass public grunting and sweating? If you prefer to work out at home, you can still take advantage of this concept by planning which workout videos you're going to do in advance. One way of doing this is by making a YouTube playlist for yourself that you can repeat every day. Or you could make a Monday Wednesday Friday video playlist and a Tuesday Thursday video playlist.

So as you can see, there's a way for you to satisfy your left brain's need for clarity and routine, while also satisfying your right brain's need for variety and creativity. And one more bonus tip: the more often you can repeat the same routine, and the less often you have to make a new routine for the same task, the better. For some things, it will make sense for you to do the same exact thing every day, and for some other things, it may make sense for you to pick one day at the end of the month or week to create the routine for the upcoming month or week. And again, if you need a little variety in your life (which we all do from time to time), give yourself scheduled off days to give your routine a rest.

Plan Ahead

One of the worst contributors to that deer-in-the-headlights-what-the-hell-do-I-do feeling when it comes to making decisions is the ticking time bomb blaring in your ear. Well, it's not actually a bomb, it's more like a clock. And of course, there's not even actually a clock, and no one can hear it but you, but it *feels* like there's a time clock blasting in your ear. Eventually, you want to get to a place where you can make good decisions under the gun. But until then, when we feel like we don't have enough time to make a good decision that we will feel confident with, stress ensues. To help mitigate this, you can plan things ahead of time.

Yes, this is where your routines can come into play for habitual things, but I'm talking more about those one-off special assignments or events. Maybe you're being presented a special award at an event and you need something special to wear. Pick it in advance. Don't wait until 11pm the night before the event to scour the city for a custom tux or ball gown. Maybe you need to conduct interviews to gather research for a special project at work. Don't pick your interviewees the morning your assignment is due. You want to make it so that when the day of your special event arrives, all of the more important details are already considered and taken care of, and all you need to do is show up.

You can also anticipate certain decisions in advance. I have a friend who's an Oscar award winning actor...in acting class. He can never actually book any meaningful acting job to show off his skills because every time he gets into the audition room, or ends up on set for a minor role, he totally freezes up and bombs. But the pity is that he could go toe to toe with the Denzel Washingtons and the Johnny Depps of the silver screen. He has it in him, but he just can't handle the pressure come game time. We often think and perform better when we are not under pressure. You can apply this concept to your decision making. Although you do not want to lay awake all night dreaming up the millions of different permutations and combinations of things that could come your way in an effort to make every one of your decisions in advance, anticipating likely decisions that you will need to make and making them in advance can be helpful.

This is similar to planning ahead, but instead of making decisions in advance for things you know are going to happen, you make decisions in advance for things you think might likely happen. When you do this for higher stress, higher stakes, and higher pressure things, when those higher stress, higher stakes, and higher pressure things come up, you'll be more calm, cool, and collected because you've already made a plan and gone through the motions in your head. You're anticipating what will likely come up and preparing yourself with your decisions in advance so that you are already prepped to make those choices and execute when the time comes.

As a small example, if you know that most times your bestie comes over for a laptop co-work day, they ask what café you want to go to, just pick one in advance so you're not wasting time when the day comes. If you often go to networking events, you know eventually someone is going to come interact with you, so have that elevator pitch ready and decide in advance what you're going to say. If you're taking the day to go car shopping and you don't yet know what you're going to get, at least decide in advance what you're looking for and what your budget is and stick to it, so you don't accidentally walk out with a yellow Ferrari convertible when you went in for a red Honda SUV. Hey, it could happen. Or, here's one that could be tied to a normal routine—if they've been doing construction off and on in your area lately, instead of rolling the dice and arriving late to work every day, pissing off your boss, and presenting your middle finger to every driver between your house and your office, just plan a detour route in advance so you can still get to work on time just in case they decide to close the roads again.

When you are anticipating decisions in advance, make sure that you are anticipating things that you are for sure expecting or things that are actually likely to happen. Avoid trying to anticipate anything that is unlikely to happen or that is not rooted in logic or reason, as this is when you can start going on that totally dreadful spiral of anxiety and overthinking about every situation that you could potentially find yourself in. Yeah sure, maybe you'll run into the Queen of England, but no need to spend time thinking about what exactly you'll say to her and how you'll push past the guards to get a selfie. So use your brain power to anticipate scenarios that are far more likely. Think a little less Queen Elizabeth run-in, and a little more construction traffic on the way to work.

So there you have it. Making choices in advance can prevent you from having that moment of surprise when the decision appears before you, as you'll already know what it is that you want. Regardless of how simple a decision may be, some of us will forever find ourselves surprised and caught off guard at even the most basic of decisions, which can lead to us struggling to make up our minds. Getting your thoughts in order ahead of time can keep you on track for what you want and can prevent you from getting the shakes and chewing your bottom lip off in the most basic of situations.

LIKE WHAT YOU SEE SO FAR?

BRAGGING ON THE INTERNET CAN SOMETIMES BE A GOOD THING.

THIS IS ONE OF THOSE TIMES.

LEAVE A REVIEW ON AMAZON, BRAGGING ABOUT HOW AWESOME YOU ARE FOR READING THIS BOOK.

CHAPTER 8

DECIDING ABOUT YOUR DECISIONS

LET'S MAKE A BET. I'm willing to bet that half the things you have swirling around your head causing you stress and decision anxiety are not even relevant right now. Did I win the bet? I feel like I won. I'm pretty sure you owe me money now. Think about it. Take a moment to think about all the areas in your life where you feel like you're at a crossroads. Now how many of those things will have a direct impact on your life right now? Not many, huh? There's something to planning ahead. It's wise and responsible to a degree. But when you're allowing yourself to be negatively emotionally and mentally affected by things in the future, that's when it becomes a problem.

Not everything needs to be decided right now. I hate procrastination—so much so that I wrote a whole book about it called *Just Do The Damn Thing*. But this is one of the few times I will give you permission to procrastinate. If you have too many decisions on your plate, especially bigger decisions, the first thing you need to decide is what to decide. Just focus on the ones that are most pressing. And once you've done that, there are three other crucial decisions you need to make around the decisions you've chosen to decide—there's a fun sentence for you.

When To Get On The Train

Deciding when to get started is one of the first things you'll need to figure out when it comes to choices involving life changes. Timing is everything. Timing alone can be the difference between something working out, and something not working out. Right person, wrong time has been the downfall of many would-be great relationships. Lying on your resume to land a software engineering job when you don't even know where the power button is on your laptop is another example of jumping the gun and choosing to try to get into something too soon.

The biggest thing you want to determine is if you are ready, and the most important way to do that is to make sure you have the capacity to do whatever it is you are debating—that includes the physical, mental, and emotional capacity. If it's a relationship, you'll want to have watched enough Oprah, scribbled through enough Moleskins, and gone to enough therapy sessions to clear out all baggage from your past and make yourself emotionally available for this new person. If it's a business, you want to have the time, money, and knowledge to start yourself off on a good foot.

Sometimes, you are going to want to do something in your life, but you first need to make sure that you have everything ready for you to get started. Attempting to get started with something before you are actually ready can lead to you ruining something that otherwise has the potential to turn out well. Sometimes, it's just a matter of sitting tight a little while longer before you choose to make a jump on something.

Now, there's something you have to remember with this. Notice I said you need to have things in place for you to *get started*, not to *finish*. When you embark upon a significant journey, you will never have everything you need to get you all the way to the finish line. It doesn't work that way. Knowledge, strategies, mentors, many things will be revealed to you along the way. You need to have the courage to take the first step...an educated, well thought out first step.

And here's the other thing that you have to remember with all this. A *big* other thing. So big that I am going to go ahead and make it its own paragraph:

There is no such thing as the perfect time.

All of the street lights are not going to turn green at the same time between here and your destination so if you're waiting on that, you're really just looking for an excuse to procrastinate. And remember, I hate procrastination. That's why I wrote *Just Do The Damn Thing*. There's a difference between waiting to quit your job until you have 6 months living expenses saved up, and telling yourself you'll start that business when your net worth rises to the level of Warren Buffet's. Newsflash, bud, your net worth will never be remotely close to what Warren

Buffet's is if you never start that business you've been sitting on.

That barista gig at Starbucks just doesn't pay 11,698,717 dollars and 95 cents an hour. So if you're telling yourself you're going to wait it out another 3 years to pad your pockets to the billions before you feel comfortable taking the leap and jumping ship on your current job, you're kidding yourself. Listen, I'm not putting down any job. Do whatever you have to do to pay your bills in the meantime. No one starts at the top. Unless you're a Kardashian. If you're not a half Armenian with a double D chest and a Jessica Rabbit cartoonish body and a waistline that would make an average 11-year-old jealous—hint, that's most of us—then you have to start somewhere. And that somewhere will likely be the bottom, which there is nothing wrong with. There's something valuable to be learned from every single experience in our lives, whether personal or professional, that will better set us up for whatever's coming up next in this thing we call life. But never ever settle or stay stuck in something you don't want for fear of pursuing what you do want.

If you feel like you are not living up to your fullest potential, chances are, what's standing between you and those elusive items on your vision board are some key decisions that you've been afraid to make and afraid to follow through on. So when you're deciding if you should start on something, and trying to figure out if you're ready, compare what you are losing by not saying "yes" now, to what you're hoping to gain for you to feel ready. Remember when we talked opportunity cost? It's not worth it for you to put off something with a potentially huge upside now because you're waiting for something to change to give you the go ahead, but that thing you're waiting on in the grand scheme of things is an itsy bitsy teeny weeny variable.

Let's say right now you have a two-year degree in Business and you want to get a four-year degree. Sure, in theory, it would be better for you to have a four-year degree. After all, basic math tells us that four is greater than two. But maybe you also right now have a mentor who's willing to take you under their wing and give you an awesome job that would put you on a fast track to success and upper level management. Go for it! This is the kind of opportunity you'd be hoping to get and qualify for after getting a four-year degree anyway. So just take it now. Instead of going to school full time to finish out that four-year degree, you can go part time while pursuing this amazing opportunity. So don't disqualify yourself over little things. Learn when you're ready *enough*, and look at the bigger picture to see if you're ready *enough* to just get started now.

And if you still need help on figuring out if you should start something or not, ask yourself these questions:

1. Have I prepared myself enough to start?
2. With the degree of preparation I have now, do I have a higher chance of success than failure? (Notice, it's not about feeling or being perfectly prepared, we just want to be over the midpoint

between likelihood for success and likelihood for failure.)

3. How high is my chance to have my desired outcome if I start right now?

4. Is there anything stopping me from feeling "ready" and is that of legitimate concern or is it imagined, blown out of proportion, or irrelevant?

5. If there were no perceived obstacles in my way, is this what I would choose?

6. If this were to go in an undesired direction, how quickly and easily would I be able to recover? (Hint--If you cussed your boss out in front of everyone in your office building, you can probably count on that job not being an option to go back to if you ever needed to)

7. Do I have a safety net in place?

8. Am I going to have the resiliency to make this work and stick through when things get hard?

9. Am I dedicated to ensuring the success of this decision?

When To Stay On The Train

You did it. You bit the bullet. You started! This calls for celebration, as most people don't get past this part. You can pat yourself on the back. But now you've been going down the path, and the path that first started as a perfectly paved, sunlit walkway now seems to be covered in gnarly vines, potholes, and trapdoors that lead to *Tomb Raider* caliber death spikes. Do you keep going, even though things are looking bleak, or do you stop now and cut your losses?

A big point of fear for many people is that they will make a choice and get involved in something, but then won't see the warning signs of when they need to change their mind and jump ship, leaving them trapped in what turned out to be a dead-end decision that they made. And it's a perfectly rational fear. In a relationship, once we're under the influence of emotions, it can be hard for us to know if the relationship is actually worth continuing or not, or if we're sticking with it because we're drunk with googly eyes or we're just plain comfortable and used to them being around by now.

Other decisions can be like that too. You may find yourself halfway down the road, and things are looking ugly, but you stay with it, not because it's right, but because you've already invested so much time, energy, and resources that you don't want it to all have been for nothing. But the opposite could also be true. You could be midway through a journey, but it gets hard, and you want to quit even though what you want is on the other side of this obstacle. Sometimes, it's not a matter of quitting altogether, it's just a matter of quitting that particular strategy that you've chosen. Sometimes, we may still want the ultimate outcome, but we just need to change up what we're doing and go about it a different way. How do you decide if you need to continue down the exact same current path, or change things up and try a new way?

Luckily, there is a way to critically think about whether it makes sense to continue with a decision or whether it is time to change your mind and choose a different course. It is possible to see the warning signs and make adjustments accordingly, so you don't feel trapped or like you're getting too carried away in the wrong direction. There's no need to stay committed to decisions that once seemed to be working, but are now causing major heartache.

Here's the thing. We tend to want to make decisions in emotionally charged moments that are not always indicative of the reality of the situation. If you're especially stoked one day for whatever reason, you're going to want to keep going. If you're feeling especially down one day for whatever reason, or someone pisses you off, you're going to want to change course or stop. To mitigate this emotional instability and the way it impedes logic, there's two things you can do. The first, is to choose in advance a particular trigger that will signal you to re-evaluate, change, or stop your current course of action.

For you, it may be if you and your spouse start fighting to the point that you're no longer sleeping in the same bed. It could be if you are no longer able to attend your kids' soccer games, or if your bank account balance gets below a certain point. Choose it in advance, when you're not actually in the situation so you won't be emotionally blinded if it does arise. The second thing you can do is choose a regular interval to do a check-in with yourself. You want to do this periodically, so you can look back at trends to give you an accurate evaluation as to whether you should continue or not.

As part of your weekly or monthly check-in, these are some great questions you can ask yourself when you are deciding whether or not it is a good idea to continue on the path you are on:

1. Do I still feel happy with my decision?
2. Have I stuck with this long enough to see any benefits from this decision?
3. Have I made any progress and positive forward movement towards my original goal?
4. Am I questioning things right now out of emotion or logic?
5. Is there anything I can change or adjust to make this decision feel or work out better?
6. Is there something I can do to change course that will lead me to my same desired outcome, but in a different way?
7. Would I benefit mentally or emotionally from a break right now? (Sometimes, for your sanity and mental and emotional rejuvenation, you don't need to stop, you just need to stop for now.)

When To Get Off The Train

Almost every decision is going to eventually have a point where it has matured and it is time for us to make a new decision. That could be the point where you have decided to quit for good, or the point where you reached your initial goal and got everything you wanted out of a particular choice, and it is now time to make a choice about what the next level is for you. Ideally, it would be the latter, but sometimes, it's the former. Knowing how to identify when a season in your life has reached the end of its cycle is an essential skill. When you can trust in yourself to recognize when it is time to call it quits on something and move on to something else, you can trust yourself so much, that making all future decisions becomes a lot easier, too. This way, you are no longer fearful that you are going to traumatize yourself by staying on the train until it crashes.

Deciding when to end something can be wrought with emotion that can make it hard to see the truth of the situation with clarity. There can be grief over what you are losing, grief over what you'd hoped to gain but never did, guilt over ending something, and shame over feeling like you weren't strong enough and didn't have what it takes to make it work. This could be a good place to consult other people who are experienced with whatever you are going through. They can not only give you encouragement, but can also give you the proper perspective to see if you are quitting too soon before you really gave it a chance.

This trusted outside perspective, coupled with your own introspection and self-reflection will help you move through the emotions of your situation without a deep and overwhelming sense of fear that leaves you feeling like you are making the wrong move. This way, you can feel confident that you don't need to question yourself or your decision out of fear of being wrong and therefore, later regretting everything.

Here are some questions you can ask yourself to help you

determine whether or not this is the right time to end something. Because this can be a bigger decision, this is a longer list of questions. You may not want or need to use all of them. You can choose which ones are best for you:

1. Am I truly ready for this to end? Why or why not?
2. Is there no other alternative to this ending?
3. If this path can potentially lead to something I want, can I truly say that I have turned over every leaf, exhausted every resource, done everything in my control to make this work out, and tried my very best?
4. If I keep going, is the likelihood of this working out positive or unlikely?
5. Can I handle the emotional repercussions of continuing with this decision?
6. Can I make some adjustments that will allow me to stay on this course and feel productive and happy?
7. Will I regret it if I stop now?
8. Do I feel nurtured and supported in this decision? (Outside unsupportive influences can make us want to quit on our goals, when really, deep down, we want to keep going.)
9. Is this starting to do me more harm than good?
10. Is the person I am (personality, disposition, values, etc) changing for the worse?
11. Is this having a negative effect on the people I care about?
12. What kind of results have I gotten so far in

comparison to the results I want? Does what I have gotten out of this feel in proportion to what I have put in?

13. Are my results typical, greater, or less compared to others at a similar stage in pursuit of a similar goal?

14. Am I willing to get help and reach out to other people who have been down the path I'm on, and am I willing to do what they say I need to do?

15. Am I gaining emotional and mental fulfilment and happiness from other areas of my life? (Whether you choose to continue this decision or not, the answer to this question needs to be yes. Having all your eggs in one happiness basket is a recipe for mental and emotional disaster, instability, and depression.)

CHAPTER 9

WHAT DO YOU MEAN THE WORLD DOESN'T REVOLVE AROUND ME??

IT'S hard enough making choices for yourself, but can be even harder when someone else is involved. When I say someone else is involved, that's not to be mistaken for the voices in your head, or the haunting memories of the people from your past who lead you to believe certain stories about yourself. I'm talking about actual humans who are physically present in your life and who may be impacted by what decisions you are making. This could be anyone from your boss or your coworkers, to your family or your friends, or a significant other. All of these people could potentially be impacted by your decisions from time to time. So sometimes you are going to have to factor others into your decisions to help you choose your outcome.

Making decisions when someone else is involved can be more challenging, as you want to ensure that you consider the other person's best interest, but you do not want to consider them to the point of dismissing your own wants and needs, especially if that becomes a habitual way of operating for you. Finding that proper balance between what you want and what they want is going to be necessary to ensure that you are not leaving out the most important part of the decision-making process—you.

The tricky thing here is to find the delicate balance between meeting both parties' needs to the best of your ability. If you are a caretaker to an elderly parent, or if you are a parent yourself, you probably find yourself in this situation often. If you really want something and you find that what you want is going to come at the expense of someone else's wellbeing, you are going to need to think long and hard about how important this actually is to you. Remember when we talked earlier about your values and principles? This is a great time to pull those suckers back out. Let your deepest values and most important principles be your guiding star in situations like this.

A similar challenge arises when you are making decisions that need to be made *with* someone else. An example of this would be picking an important plan of action with a business partner or choosing to buy a house with a romantic partner. Knowing how to make decisions *with* other people is just as important as knowing how to make decisions that are going to impact other people so that you are effectively making choices in a way that is going to benefit everyone involved.

If you have a partner, you want to do what's best for you, but remembering that there are two people in a relationship, you want to always talk to your partner about the decision, out of respect for them. Whether it's a personal, romantic, or professional relationship, people appreciate feeling included, heard, and considered in the decision process. When you're a part of a relationship, you're a part of a team. Every time it comes time for you to make a choice that could potentially impact the both of you, you want to talk with your partner about it—not to be confused with telling them about it and briefing them on what you've already decided. The my-way-or-the-highway approach doesn't exactly lend itself to healthy, happy partnerships. Not only does it feel like crap to be on either end of that, but it will also lead to people casting you out of their lives eventually because they feel unappreciated and disrespected. You don't want to become *that* person. You just don't.

This is what I love about being single. Sure, I have to pay for my own dinners and rely on the kindness of strangers for compliments, but my decisions are made by me and for me only, and there's no one else to consider. It's a heck of a lot less complicated that way. But if you are in some sort of a partnership, not only do you need to make up your own mind but you also need to make your decision align with the other person so that you are able to move forward in a mutually beneficial way. Sometimes, making decisions with other people can be especially challenging because neither of you are on the same page, so you have a hard time committing to anything that you want.

If you come to a decision dead-lock with someone else, you first of all, need to both be open and willing to talk it through and find a solution, which is something that not everyone is always willing to do. Sometimes, it can be easier to stay at odds and avoid the tough conversations than it is to actually collaborate and try to come up with a solution, especially when it's at the risk of upsetting someone or worse, ruining the relationship. If you start by being willing to come to a solution and declaring that to the other person, your own will can help the other person become more open to the idea of finding a resolution as well.

Next, you are going to need to both know what your values are and what you want long term. It's imperative that you're both clear on that and willing to speak your truth on it, not just saying what you think the other person wants to hear. Then, you must both be willing to compromise and negotiate, as you may both need to wiggle some on your position so that you can find a mutual stance. When you go into negotiations, know your deal breakers, so you won't risk giving way too much to the point that it's not good for you.

When it comes to other people being involved, your decisions can be win lose, or they can be win win. One person should not always be the winner. And the same person should not always be the loser either. It's ideal if every decision ends up being win win, but that's not always realistic or possible. Sometimes, someone is going to get the short end of the stick. But the same person shouldn't be drawing the short straw every time, whether that's the other person, or you.

Also keep in mind that a decision that starts off as a win, could potentially not end up that way. In other words, the impact of your choices can be one thing in the immediate short term, but could be something completely different in the long term. Same decision, different impact as you follow it down through time. So remember to look at the big picture.

You want to make it a priority to consider other peoples' wellbeing while still making the right decision for yourself. A big problem presents itself when people stop making decisions for themselves because they are afraid that speaking up for what they think or want will push the other person away. In the long run, this suppression of your own desires can lead to resentment and frustration in your relationships and your life.

Compromise is the key to any solid relationship, but the thing you need to realize is that at the end of the day, you are the one who has to live with the decisions you have made, even if they are decisions made with or on behalf of other people. All the weight of these decisions is going to fall on your shoulders, and you need to be ready to handle that weight. Otherwise, you are going to find yourself living in a life that you feel was not meant for you, miserable, and constantly looking for a way out. And when you do finally reach the point where you can no longer handle the commitment, leaving the life you have made for yourself is now going to cause even more strain for you and the other person involved.

If you were in a long term relationship with someone and

you had to decide whether to move to a different city for a job opportunity for your partner, this is a decision that would uproot your life. It may require you to move away from your closest friends, your family, and even sacrifice your own career. All of these things need to be considered so you don't end up miserable. And get creative. Look at what the root of the desired outcome is, and brainstorm from there. Sometimes the answer could be an answer that you cannot initially see. Perhaps the solution is for you both to stay put and for your partner to find a remote job, or start a business so that moving is no longer a requirement. You get to stay close to your loved ones and keep your job, while they still get what they want, just in a different package. They still get a better professional opportunity and career advancement. So initially, it seemed like your only options were to stay or go, but if you look deeper and harder, you can come up with a creative solution.

So allow yourselves to step back and see if there are any other solutions that you can come up with. You may find that the present options being presented to you are not something that you can agree on, but if you collaborate and think hard enough, you may find that there is an alternative that you can both come together on that helps you stay on the same page and move forward as a united unit. That creative solution may not initially be obvious, and trying to reach a compromise can sometimes get heated, so if necessary, give each other a fixed amount of time and space to give you both room to figure out a new and better idea.

CHAPTER 10

CHANGE YOUR MIND AROUND CHANGING YOUR MIND

ALLOW ME TO MAKE A SUGGESTION—CHANGE the way you think and the way you look at this whole thing. This whole decision making thing is so hard for you because you're putting way too much pressure on yourself and taking things way too seriously. Fortunately for you, there are many ways that you can overcome your indecisiveness and get on with your life already by simply changing your perspective around how you are seeing the very decisions that you are faced with. Let's dig into eight different simple perspective shifts that you can take advantage of that will help you start making life choices with greater accuracy and speed, and help you to chill out a little bit.

You're Not Aristotle

First things first. It's not that deep. So stop turning everything into some metaphorical, philosophical, what-is-the-meaning-of-life moment. You are not Aristotle for crying out loud, so there is no reason why you should have to assign such depth and meaning to every single little thing that you do. Sure, you may want everything to have some deeper and more mysterious meaning in your life, but the reality is that most things truly are superficial and do not carry nearly as much weight as you think they do.

Just because you and your crush are both Capricorns and you both like *Game of Thrones*, it doesn't mean they're your soulmate. Just because you don't wear a tie to work, it doesn't mean you won't get taken seriously or will get passed over for a promotion. If you get passed over for a promotion, trust me, it wasn't the tie. It very well might have been the fact that you show up a half hour late every day to work because you spend so much time at home agonizing over if you should wear a tie or not. But believe me, it's not the tie itself. Just because you went to the grocery store today and chose to purchase a cereal with marshmallows in it over that granola bran rabbit food cereal, it does not mean that you have signaled to the cutie standing in the aisle next to you that you are some Diabetes-bound man-child who will never succeed in life. There is no deeper meaning. Today, you wanted the sugary cereal, so you bought the sugary cereal, period. Hearts, stars, and horseshoes, clovers, and blue moons make your heart sing. So today, Lucky Charms won.

So stop thinking that everything has some deep mysterious meaning and start seeing things for what they truly are by looking at situations objectively without the added narrative in your head about what it all means for you, your future, your future children, and your future children's children. Most day-to-day decisions are just not that deep.

Who Cares, Anyway?

I'll tell you who—no one. Well, correction—you. Mostly just you.

Chances are at this point you have a list a mile long of the people you are concerning yourself with based on what you believe their opinions of you will be whenever you make a decision. You may find yourself mentally scrolling through that list to make sure that everyone approves of everything you do before you do it, even if they are not around to actually witness you making said decision. You could be on autopilot, making certain choices because of what you've heard people say in the past, without ever even stopping to think about whether or not you agree, or if those people even actually care about what choices you are making.

Did you decide not to wear that stunning low neckline dress to your wedding because Aunt Lucy used to be a nun? Do you find yourself spending extra time choosing what to wear in Q4 because your Grandma said once that she never wears white after Labor Day? I mean, do you really think that Grandma is going to get into hand-to-hand combat with you because you decided to wear your white tennis shoes in October? No, give it up. Grandma does not care. And if Grandma is on the other side now, trust me, she's definitely not coming to haunt you and throw bad karma on your day because you wore white.

Beyond the people in your head who you are narrating for, the people around you likely do not care about what you are doing, either. Again, your decisions are not that deep. Most of them don't say much about you and if they do, more often than not, no one is even listening anyway. I mean, so what you ordered an espresso at six in the evening. Do you really think the guy on his cell phone standing behind you cares? No. Stop worrying about what everyone else thinks and start worrying about what you care about since it will be *you* who needs to live with the results of your decisions anyway. There is no sense in living a life that you are miserable with because you are far too concerned with what other people want to make a decision for yourself.

We often get so caught up in the little things out of fear and concern for what other people may think. What we forget is that most people will not be judging what you're wearing, what you decide to do with your hair, or what career path you choose because they'll be too concerned with being afraid that you are judging them.

Commit. For Now.

If you are holding yourself back because you have a chronic need to see everything ten to twenty years out in the future, you need to knock that right the heck off. No, buying a red car today does not mean that you will be driving that same exact red car in twenty years. No, choosing lasagna over spaghetti does not mean that you will never taste spaghetti again. No, going on a date with a person that your friend sets you up with does not mean that you are going to get married and have twelve kids and three dogs with them on a farm somewhere in Oklahoma. No, choosing to take a job that you do not particularly like for a pay increase does not mean that you are going to be strapped to the hip of that same soul-sucking corporation for the rest of your life.

The decisions that you make today can definitely impact your future, but they are not going to impact it quite as much as you think, or not as long term as you think. We act like every decision we make locks us in, sets things in stone, and etches the outcome into the fabric of history. We act as if each and every little decision brings with it a permanent outcome. You are not making a decision for the rest of your life. You are making a decision for now. So it's pointless to spend so much time ruminating over everything.

So if you are struggling to make choices because you have lied to yourself and created this illusion that you need to stick with it forever, you need to relax. Dial back your intensity a notch or two, and realize that it is perfectly fine for you to make a choice right now and then go ahead and change your mind later on. No one is going to punish you because you chose to change your mind.

Getting all worked up because you think that every choice you make means that you need to be committed to it until the end of time is a waste of your energy, and quite frankly, when it comes to the little things, it makes you look like a doofus. It's an ice cream flavor, not a husband.

It's a t-shirt color, not a wife. You're not getting married to it forever. Just frickin pick one.

What You See Isn't Always What You Get

Here's the thing. You can do everything right and still be totally wrong, and you can do everything wrong and still end up totally right. I know, it sounds so screwed up, doesn't it? But it's true. Many times, we fear making decisions because we think we are going to get it wrong, so we put so much effort and time into trying to get everything absolutely perfect, only to later find that it was wrong anyway. Or, we're on the right track with something, and try so hard to make sure it ends up right, but in doing so, we mess everything up. Or, we do not put enough focus into a decision, so we do what appears to be screwing it up, only to find out later on that we still ended up getting it right anyway.

Life is a crazy thing, and it doesn't always make sense to us. Our decisions can often go in ways that we totally do not expect. Learning to understand that you do not have the answer key to life can help you start making decisions in good faith, trusting that everything is going to work out in the long run. Being afraid of doing everything wrong is not going to guarantee that you do everything right, so there is no sense overwhelming yourself with these fears to the point where you cannot even make up your mind in the first place.

If you are still totally screwed up about screwing everything up, and are convinced that you're going to make a decision that will ruin your life, focus on being okay with making the right decision for the moment based on the information that you currently have. Rather than trying to get everything right long-term, be okay with figuring it out as you go and making decisions with the knowledge that you have. As more information shows up, you can always exercise your right to change your mind as you go, so do not feel like you only have one chance to make everything right. Instead, realize that you are always doing the best that you can and that there are plenty of opportunities for you to grow and do better in the future, even if you do screw it up right now. Not that you will.

Remember this: life tends to favor action over inaction. Taking a step is almost always better than standing still. Moving, even if in the wrong direction, is better than not moving at all in any direction. The good news is: you can correct course along the way. When it comes to life decisions, you will get feedback along the way as you move forward. You don't have to have the whole course plotted out perfectly before you start.

A torpedo arrives at its target by making countless mistakes. It will make it to its destination by essentially making a series of tiny errors and a series of tiny corrections of those errors, but when you zoom out and look at the big picture, it looks like it was heading in an exact perfectly executed path towards its target the whole time. But it wasn't. The torpedo isn't scared to be deployed. It's not scared to get out there. It's not scared to start or make the first move. And it's not scared to make a mistake because that's ultimately how it ends up where it wants to go in the first place. Be more like the torpedo.

Screws Can Be Unscrewed

Did anybody die?

Ok, then we can fix it.

In the event that you do totally screw something up, you need to stop thinking that everything is finite and final. Just like the outcome is not final if you make a choice, the outcome is not final if you make a choice and totally eff it up. Believe it or not, there is almost always a perfectly fine answer to all of your problems, and any screw up you make can almost always be fixed or at least minimized by changing your mind, altering your course of action, and taking appropriate actions later on.

Just because you make a mistake does not mean that you are some horrible person and that you have irreversibly screwed up your own life and the lives of everyone around you. Instead, it simply means that you are a human who made a mistake and that you are learning... *surprise!* That's right: even if people are frustrated with you in the short term, rarely will people truly hold a mistake against you and try to make you pay for it for the rest of your life, unless they are totally screwed up people themselves. In that case, screw them. And likewise, if you make a mistake, you shouldn't hold it against yourself and try to make yourself pay for it for the rest of your life. If you're doing that, then screw you...well, you're actually already screwing yourself.

Don't do yourself a disservice convincing yourself that no problem is fixable. If you make a mistake, you can simply learn how to undo the mistake. You can *Control + Z* your way right back on the right track. In the end, it will help you have a greater understanding of how freaking strong you are, and how resourceful and adaptable you are. And it will give you the added confidence that you are capable of fixing your mistakes, plus you'll learn how you can avoid making the same mistake in the future. In the end, it will totally not be as bad as you think it will be and you can continue on with your life knowing that you are not a total screw up and yes, the people in your life do still love you, and you can still love yourself even if you messed up once or twice.

If everyone is still alive, it's fixable. And when it comes to most of your decisions, nobody's going to die...unless of course you give yourself a stroke from stressing out over which decision you're going to make.

Life University

Seeing your mistakes as a learning experience is valuable, but you can take it a step further and see the entire decision-making process as a learning experience if you really want to get into the positive vibes of life. In life, every single choice you make opens up the opportunity for you to learn more about yourself, about life, and about the people that you are sharing your life with.

You'll not only learn the obvious like your likes and dislikes, but if you dig deeper, you'll gain insight into your values, your strengths, your weaknesses, your limitations, and your deepest pains. That way, you'll be able to make decisions in the future based on your values, make improvements to your areas of weakness, consciously push past your limitations the next time they show up, and clear out suppressed emotions brewing from your past.

When you're making a choice and you have resistance to that choice, you can ask yourself why, and take yourself all the way down the chain of why's until you've ended up in a puddle of your own tears after having essentially served as your own personal therapist. For instance, let's say you're trying to decide if you should wear that coverup or shirt to the beach, or just be free in your bikini or loud and proud in your speedo. If you take yourself down the chain of why's, you may find that you were feeling uncomfortable about your body and felt the need to cover it up because way back when, someone you had feelings for made fun of your body for the way it looked and you've been self-conscious and dressed overly modestly ever since.

You've opened up a wound, sure, but you've uncovered an opportunity for self-exploration, self-healing, and new information that can make similar kinds of decisions easier in the future. As another example, if you ask yourself why you're making a decision, and the answer is out of fear, you can choose to make that decision anyway and overcome that fear. Now, you've used the decision-making process to push past a former limitation and grow.

See, when you come into the decision-making process with curiosity in mind, you begin to see how you can make the most out of every single choice. You end up staying open to learning about how your decisions reflect on who you are and you discover your own perspective, and get to know you, all of which will make future decisions even easier. Choosing to see your decision-making process as a learning experience rather than a totally freaky situation that is driving stakes of anxiety through your entire body can be quite valuable. You can approach the whole thing with curiosity instead of fear, which can help you have even more success with making decisions with greater ease.

It's All A Part Of The Process

Part of getting yourself off your own back when it comes to making decisions is realizing that everything is a part of your process in life. People who do not make decisions go nowhere, which is why you need to be willing to put effort into choosing a direction and going with it if you are going to generate any level of happiness in life. I mean think about it, if you were faced with a decision and you never made it, where would you end up? You would not move forward or backward, you would just stay exactly where you are with no hope for advancement. Staying firmly rooted in one place forever is certainly no way to live unless you are a tree, in which case, be my guest. But if you're not about that tree life, you need to give yourself the opportunity to grow through everything that comes your way by being willing to make a choice and move on in life, whether that move is forward, backward, or sideways. In the bigger picture, every move is a positive move because it always brings something positive into your life, whether it's a person, an experience, or a lesson.

Sometimes, you may make a decision and end up totally bummed out about it. You might move across the country to be with a great partner who you love only to find out they are a total jackass in their home state. As a result, you might stick around and potentially meet the person you're actually supposed to be with. Or, you'll move back, but will take with you the new friends and positive memories (jackass not included), and the knowledge and confidence that you had the courage to take a leap of faith.

Either way, you win. And either way, neither positive outcome would have occurred had you not first made that initial decision. You learned about yourself, you experienced life, and you went on a magnificent journey that allowed you to grow forward through everything that came your way. This is a wonderful way for you to realize that life can be totally freaking amazing, even if you find out in the long run that some decisions that you made turned out to be the wrong decisions for you. Through regularly making these choices in the first place, you end up finding your way to what is right for you, thus meaning that every choice you make, whether it is right or wrong, is leading you forward. You just never know when one of these choices is going to lead you to a life-changing experience that you have been craving all your life.

So respect the order and the mysterious ways of life. Respect the process. As each piece unfolds, you advance towards the destination. Just like with a road trip or a movie, in life, you can't just skip to the end. And if you could, where would the fun be in that?

There Are Multiple Ways To 18

3 X 6 is 18.

2 X 9 is also 18.

Or, you could choose to put the 9 first, and 9 X 2 also happens to be 18.

You know what else? 1 X 18 is also 18.

Why are we going back to second grade and doing times tables right now? To prove a point. I'm sorry if I conjured up PTSD flashbacks from elementary school math class, but this is an important one. The eighth and final change you need to make to your mindset comes down to understanding that there is always more than one path towards your desired outcome. If you were hiking in the woods, and you came to a fork in the path, and it split into 7 different directions, how would you feel? Add to that that the sun is setting and you hear howling in the distance. Now, how do you feel? Probably a little stressed, naturally. You know where you want to go, but you have no idea which way to pick because you have no clue which way leads you to your desired destination. But what if you came to that same fork in the path and there was a sign that indicated that all 7 paths lead to the same place? Doesn't that take a load off?

We tend to get so caught up in creating our "right path forward" and fighting so desperately to make things unfold exactly the way we have in mind that we forget the bigger picture and the most important thing. There's no need to stress over which path to take. In the end, there are often many ways that we can get to where we desire to go, as long as we are willing to take action to actually get there.

Remember our math example. There are many different ways you can get to the number 18. And we just did multiplication. That's not even counting the multitude of other ways you could get to 18. You could also do addition (11 + 7 is 18), subtraction (23 − 5 is 18), division (180 / 10 is 18)...we could get real fancy and start doing calculus and trigonometry, but I didn't do well in those classes in school, so you'll have to live with my basic algebra examples.

But the point is every single one of these equations will equal 18, therefore meaning they are *all* the right answer. So if someone asks you how to make 18 and you're sweating bullets like someone's holding a gun to your head, you're having a coronary for no good reason, pal. There are multiple paths that you can take to get to the same end. So when it comes to making decisions in life, you can mentally come back to this unwanted math lesson. The key is understanding that there is no single right path forward and that you are going to need to just pick one that feels right for you and trust that it will somehow take you where you need to go.

There is a popular saying that goes "the only path that will end in failure is the one that ends too soon," meaning that if you are unwilling to keep trying until you succeed, that's how you ensure failure. And if you learn to see each apparent "failure" in your life as guidance in the right direction, then surely you will find your success eventually. By just picking a step forward and then taking it, whether it seems like the right step or not, then consistently continuing to move, you ensure that you will eventually get to where you need to go. This way, you don't make like a tree and stand still, but instead you get your ass in gear and start taking big action towards your goal, and as a result, you make progress in your life.

CHAPTER 11

PICK YOUR POISON

HOW DO you get out of the pain of decision making? Don't make a decision. There. Problem solved.

Not so fast.

Not picking anything is often worse than picking something that you thought was the "wrong" thing because not picking anything can still lead to you experiencing unwanted consequences, *and* it can rob you of a potential lesson that can lead you to the right thing, *and* because you've chosen to stay at a standstill, you don't get any further ahead in getting what you want out of life. And even though it doesn't seem like it, not picking anything is in fact a choice as well.

You think making a decision is painful? There are four different pains you will have to deal with if you don't make a decision—the pain of resistance, the pain of incompletion, the pain of regret, and the pain of imperfection. Not making a decision and as a result, facing one or more of the Four Pains is much more painful than making a choice. So if you don't make a choice, you're essentially choosing one of the Four Pains instead. Once you see how painful these can be, it will hopefully put into perspective for you how little the pain of making a decision is by comparison. So pick your poison. I suggest pushing through the pain of making a decision. Trust me, it definitely beats all the Four Pains.

The Pain Of Resistance

If you don't make a choice, you will be stuck with the pain of resistance. That inner feeling of constantly feeling tugged in different directions. Doubting your every thought and your every move. Not trusting yourself or having full confidence in yourself. Keeping yourself back from making a move because you don't have faith in your own ability to choose the right move. Feeling constantly unsettled and at war with yourself.

The pain of resistance truly is the pain of indecisiveness itself. Resistance leads to analysis paralysis, avoidance, and denial. And that's not even the worst of it. It's bad enough losing confidence in yourself and being in a tumultuous mental state. But the true trouble with resistance lies in what happens in the long term. The thing about resistance is that the longer you resist something, the easier it becomes for you to stay in resistance.

When it comes to decisions, this means that the longer you allow yourself to stay in this painful state of decision limbo, the more apt you are to carry that same pattern of behavior over to other subsequent decisions. And you're ultimately making it easier and easier for you to avoid making choices because decision neglect becomes your natural mode of operation. Many people find themselves trapped in resistance mode because what can start with resistance to one decision can rapidly grow into triggering a resistance response for all decisions, causing further difficulty processing information and creating a new source of anxiety.

The reality is, when we do not decide because we are resisting the necessity to make a choice, we are often making the worst choice possible. You may think that you could not possibly do anything worse than making the wrong decision, but that could not be any further from the truth. Virtually every single time you make no decision at all, you have made the worst decision that you could have possibly made and you are the only one to blame for that.

See, when you do not decide what you want in life, you literally make yourself powerless. You take away your opportunity to choose the next step for yourself in life, and you place that opportunity directly in someone else's hands. That's how it works. Decisions will be made. They'll either be made *by* you or *for* you. When you don't make a choice, someone else will step in and make the choice for you, then you'll be subject to the outcome of what they've decided. Would you rather take your chance on someone else's choice or your own?

The Pain Of Incompletion

There's a reason why we feel like we need closure after the

end of a relationship. There's a reason why you sleep easier when the door to your house is closed and locked instead of wide open. There's a reason why you feel like you can't stop a Netflix binge sesh in the middle of an episode. There's a reason why most people want to finish their school degrees. There's a reason why you feel bad when you quit something. Leaving things unfinished and open ended takes up mental space. They sit on the backburner of our minds, slowing nagging at us, burning a hole in our brains, and we wonder why we can't focus on anything.

Incompletion not only gets in the way of a clear head, but it carries with it feelings of guilt and pain—guilt that we didn't fulfill a commitment, and pain that we're not the kind of person that's able to fulfill a commitment. There's the feeling you have to carry with yourself of being a non-finisher. It's not a good feeling knowing that you can't count on yourself to see something through to the end.

And it's an even worse feeling wondering if something could have turned out better if you'd just stuck with it a little longer. Don't get me wrong—not everything is meant to last forever. Sometimes, things are a dead end, and you need to jump off the train before it crashes with you on it. But some things, you just plain quit too soon to give it a fair chance at a positive outcome. And if you're honest with yourself, you'll see that that's likely the more common scenario.

In life, there comes a time where you have to stop being so wishy-washy about everything and start following through on your decisions so that you can see their results. You're going to have to stop worrying that everything is going to end tragically wrong and start believing that if things can work out for other people, they can work out for you too... as long as you actually see things through. Some people reach this point organically when they realize that their life is a total wasteland of missed opportunities and bad excuses, and they come to understand that the real reason their life doesn't look the way they want it to is that they never see anything through. They lose the trust and confidence of their peers, their loved ones, their friends, and themselves because they're constantly going back and forth on everything that they say they're going to do.

Incomplete decisions often lead to distress within yourself in the end. When it comes to something you should have done, you'll know. You'll feel like you should have finished it, and you will find yourself upset that you did not feel brave or committed enough to follow through on the promise that you made. Not only will you have to deal with those feelings of incompetence within yourself, but you will also have to face other people around you who have been pulled into your decisions until that point.

You will find that each time you do this, things becomes harder and harder as you begin to identify yourself with being the kind of person who never finishes a project that they have committed to. Soon, this identity will consume you, and you will find yourself always expecting that you fall short on commitments. And you start to expect for things to not work, but really, if you look back on it closely, you'll see that you never really gave anything a chance to work because you never saw anything through. Something left half done hurts. Half pursued relationships and half pursued dreams make for a half ass life.

The Pain Of Regret

This is perhaps the most painful of all the Four Pains. You don't want to get to the end of your life and realize that you didn't get to do or experience what you wanted. Yet that's what happens when you allow yourself to live a life dictated by the pain of regret. The pain of having to think about what could have been, what should have been, what would have been, if we had just chosen differently—or chosen at all, really—is one of the most difficult pills to swallow. Just ask the dying. That's what Australian nurse Bronnie Ware did, and then she wrote a book about it.

Ware worked in palliative care and had the opportunity to spend people's last few weeks on earth with them. During this time, she was able to get to know them intimately, and she discovered that the most common regret of the dying was that people wished they'd lived their lives true to themselves instead of living the life other people expected of them. Essentially, the biggest regret that people had were the things they chose not to do. When people get to the end of their lives, they most regret the things they didn't do, not the things they did do. What does that tell you? The most pain they feel is from decisions they *didn't* make, not decisions they *did* make.

Think of the last time you chose not to do something and you were left wrestling with "what ifs"? What if that cutie in class was the one that got away because you were too afraid to walk up to them and start a conversation? What if that solar powered portable hot dog bun warmer was the idea that could have made you a multi-millionaire? It's when we decide *not* to do things that we usually have regrets. It hurts far more to not know how something could have turned out, to know that things could have been better, you could have gotten what you wanted, had you just had the courage to make a choice to do something. That pain is much greater than the pain of picking something. So don't wait until you get on your deathbed to ask that cutie out or start a business. It's a little late then, pal.

We don't have forever to play this game called life. One day, it'll be game over. Sometimes it takes this kind of perspective to shake the fear of making a decision on something. While you're sitting over here mulling over a decision, petrified to make a choice, your life and your opportunities are saying sayonara, and passing you right on by. The things that we think are big and scary today, when we look back in the rearview mirror, we can see how small and insignificant they actually are.

When you are faced with a big decision, try to zoom out and mentally move back. Better yet, try to mentally move forward. When you get far enough down the line mentally, and you get to the end of your life, how do you think you'll feel about this decision you're wrestling with right now? Will it seem like as big a deal in 60 years as it does today? Will the stakes seem as high when you look at it from that far in the future?

Think right now about your own choices. Conjure up those old memories, rewind the tapes, go back in the ol' archives, rustle through the ol' memory bank, and think about your life up until this point that you are at right now. Everything that has happened in your life is a result of the decisions that you have made. Each decision resulted in a particular outcome and led you to where you are right now. Think for a moment. How many of the decisions that you've made have resulted in positive outcomes? You wouldn't have experienced any of those good outcomes had you not made a choice. Now think, how many of the decisions that you made resulted in unfavorable outcomes? I'll give you a sec to think...And after some time elapsed, how many of those unfavorable outcomes turned out to somehow lead you to a favorable outcome after all?

When you look back, and you weigh the number of decisions that turned out well against the number of decisions that didn't, you'll see that you're practically batting a thousand. Most of the choices you make work out. When we choose to make a move in a direction towards what we ultimately want or envision for our lives, the thing is, it usually turns out well, even if indirectly or down the line in the future where you just can't see the full benefits of the outcome yet from your point of view in the present moment.

The irony is that when it comes to the pain of regret, most people are motivated by avoiding regret. but they actually end up causing the very regret they were trying to avoid because they are too afraid to make a choice and move forward, causing them to miss out. Maybe they think on a past decision that had a less than savory outcome, so they use that as evidence for them to not make a similar decision. People do this all the time with relationships. They have one bad relationship with one particular douchebag who happens to have red hair, and now all future redheads are punished and met with death stares. Or maybe they've sworn off all relationships entirely, having written off the entire gender as being doucheville.

It makes sense to learn from past mistakes. That's how our basic survival instinct works. We encounter a neutral situation, it turns out not to be so neutral after all, it sucks, we get hurt, we make a conscious choice not to do that thing again. This kind of logic can help you keep yourself out of sticky situations, but it's not meant to keep you out of *every* situation. When it comes to certain things, you have to be okay with treating it as a new and separate situation. You can't treat everything as if it's the exact same and you're not going to enjoy life much if you treat everything like it's covered in yellow caution tape.

The Pain Of Imperfection

This one is a little different than the other three pains in that instead of being a pain that you feel if you don't make a decision, it's a pain that you have to get over in order to make a decision in the first place. To the perfectionist, the idea of not doing something perfect just plain hurts. Wanting to do things right and do things perfectly can be completely crippling and cause you to not do anything at all. And it emotionally hurts to intellectually know that you should make a move, but you mentally can't.

Sometimes it's tied to our ego. We may feel the need to protect our identity as the person who always does things well. We don't want to make a wrong move and put our reputation in jeopardy, putting the favorable way that people see us at risk. Or, maybe the opposite is true. Maybe we're tired of being known as the screw up, so we feel the need to be perfect because we want to prove ourselves. Maybe perfectionism is so ingrained in our personal identity that our pride and ego just want the satisfaction of feeling that we executed something to perfection.

Perfectionism can very commonly come from a fear of doing something wrong and experiencing a negative outcome. But that fear doesn't ever take into account the irreversibility of nearly every decision. That fear also fails to take into account the fact that there's no such thing as perfect. But when we think in this limiting way, it is operating under the assumption that there is only one good and correct way to do something. And that is simply not the case. But no matter the reason, perfectionism can be crippling, and quite frankly, it's not worth it. Trying to do and be perfect is just not worth the mental and emotional strain it causes, and certainly not worth the regret you're setting yourself up for.

One way to get over this is to stop being so hard on others. That's right, I said stop being so hard on *others*. You may have been expecting me to say something that has something to do with you, but your perfectionism has everything to do with the way you see other people. If you are the perfectionistic type of person, you probably very harshly judge other people for their shortcomings and apparent imperfections. You probably pick other people apart and look down on them when you think they're not doing things right, whether that means not making the right life choices, or not doing things in the right way in your eyes.

If you weren't so hard on other people, you wouldn't feel the need to be so hard on yourself. And when you're not so hard on yourself, you end up not being as hard on other people. It's a positive cycle that starts with you taking it easy on others. Sometimes, if you're too tight-wound with perfectionism, it can be hard to start with easing up on yourself, so start with others and let the positive cycle run its course.

When you plague yourself with perfectionism in the decision-making process, you stop yourself from moving forward on things that have potentially positive outcomes. Imagine if you wanted to launch a business that you were super passionate about. Maybe you don't even have to imagine it. Maybe that's true for you. You're totally stoked by the idea of this business, and you want to get started. But you find yourself getting hung up on the business plan, trying to get the logo just right, designing the products absolutely perfectly...all of the little decisions keep you held up and prevent progress because you can't pick anything so you can't move forward.

Look at the iPhone right now. Is it the same as the first model that came out over ten years ago? Absolutely not. But if Steve Jobs was waiting on it to be absolutely perfect, it never would have made it to market at all. Things don't have to be perfect right out of the gate. You just take your best shot and make improvements and adjustments along the way. There is no such thing as perfect. There may be a "perfect for now" scenario, but there is no such thing as perfect. "Good enough" is the best you're going to get. And most of the time, a "good enough" decision is good enough to get you where you want to go.

So many people die with their dreams and ideas inside of them because they're petrified of doing things "wrong." Don't be one of those people. Being hard on yourself because you are not an immediate expert in something is like being hard on yourself because you booked a ticket to Italy for the first time, and you weren't instantaneously fluent in Italian by the end of your first day in Italy. Holding this unreasonably high standard on yourself is only ever going to keep you from taking action on doing the things that you love because you are always going to feel incapable and unworthy. Rather than seeing that you are just a beginner learning the ropes, or giving yourself the freedom to figure things out as you go along, you are going to think that you are some bogus, incompetent dingbat who cannot seem to get anything right. Believe me when I say that the only person who gives a crap about your perfection is you, which means you are the only thing standing in the way of your own joy and happiness. So don't just stand there. Get the heck out of the way!

CHAPTER 12

YOU DON'T HAVE TO

DO you want to know a major cheat code for eliminating the stress around making decisions? Clear your plate. No, I'm not telling you to eat more. I'm telling you to do less. I'm telling you to make it so that fewer things end up on your to do list and your regular schedule. Clearing things out of your schedule can drastically reduce the number of run-ins with the decisions you have to make. The less you do, the fewer choices you have to make. Simple as pie. *Mmm...pie.*

Are you stressed because you have to choose if you want blue cupcakes with white frosting or white cupcakes with blue frosting for the neighborhood watch club meeting? Are you losing sleep at night over whether you should choose eggshell or alabaster as the background color for the Save the Whales flyers? Are you your friend's maid of honor, and now you're essentially stuck planning someone else's wedding when planning your own nearly got you admitted to the psych ward? I'm not saying be selfish and never do anything for the benefit for any other human being. But I am saying don't overcommit yourself to things that you can't physically, mentally, or emotionally give your all to.

So you can find your cause—one cause—and stick to that. And you can let it be known to your friends what kinds of requests you're good for and which ones you're not. Don't say yes to everything. Don't be that person or that friend who gets stuck with doing everything because everyone knows you'll say yes. If you don't want to be on the committee, don't be on the committee. If you don't want to sign up, don't sign up. If you don't want to say yes, don't say yes. But what a lot of us end up doing out of guilt or out of over concern for what other people will think of us, is not only signing up, but also taking on a leadership role. So now all of a sudden, you've found yourself Chairman and Treasurer of the Alliance of French Bulldogs and the People Who Love Them, so you're spending your spare time negotiating city permits for Frenchie Fest instead of figuring out if you should go with Google or Amazon for that new job offer.

You need to get a grip on what it is that you *actually* care about in your life. Not the things you want it to look like you care about. Not the things you want other people to think you care about. Not the things that make you feel guilty if you don't pretend to care about. I'm just talking about what you actually care about. This can include people, hobbies, and causes. If you are constantly doing a bunch of meaningless (or even meaningful) crap because you feel like you have to, you are going to find yourself completely overwhelmed.

Over time, all of the little meaningless (or meaningful) shit will accumulate into a giant shit snowball that will run you over before you know it, leaving you not only squished, but also feeling overwhelmed and unavailable for the most important things for you, which means that you are making your life unnecessarily challenging. By continuing to choose to take on extra tasks from your friends, family, or colleagues and growing your to do list nonstop in favor of everyone else around you, you are overwhelming yourself in highly unnecessary ways and causing anxiety. And boy oh boy, does anxiety suck. And it sucks enough for me to have written a book about it called *Chill Out Bro*. If you want to chill out, it's time to separate the wheat from the chaff and get that personal schedule and to do list under control.

Put Your Priorities To Paper

Prioritize what needs to get done. The best way to do this is to sit down and write or type what needs to get done and when. Begin writing down every single thing that you have committed to as it relates to every role that you play in your life. Write every decision that (you think) you need to make, and every task that is weighing on you and get that out of your head. Then, go ahead and start organizing that list based on your priorities of what actually matters and what does not. Rank everything on that list by priority by putting a number next to it. Then you'll be able to see everything from what is the most important overall to what is the least important overall so that you can start getting a feel for what actually needs to be done. You will likely be surprised to find that, despite how overwhelmed and clunky your brain feels right now, there is not nearly as much in the "red alert" category as you thought there would be. This is the first step towards letting yourself off the hook for shit you never wanted to do anyway.

Ditch That Crap

Now that you have prioritized the list, you need to start moving through it to get an idea of what is no longer needed in your life. Get really clear on what you can let go of and what you can completely cut out of your life altogether so that you are not holding on to any unnecessary commitments. This is not just about things that need to be done, but this is about decisions that you have already made but are now regretting in your life. So yes, you might break a few hearts, but you're just going to have to step down as president of the *Tiger King* Fan Club if it's in your best interest.

For other more important decisions, especially ones that involve other people, look at how close to the end you are to seeing it through and how close the person you committed to is to you. If you've already planned your BFF's bachelor party and all that's left to do is forward an invoice, don't stop now, just finish it. But allowing yourself to back away slowly from some of the unwanted decisions that you've made is a great way to take off your

Superman's cape and relieve some of the stress in your life and clear your head.

Give It Back

Now that you've cut a bunch of crap from your list, time to see what you can give away. Some things you won't be able to completely leave undone, but you can't realistically handle them either, so, time to delegate. Find someone else willing to do it, allow someone to help or to take over, or return it to the original sender. If you are a people pleaser or a perfectionist, admitting that you cannot do it all and trying to get some help up in here might be challenging because it may feel like you are a total failure. It is not uncommon for people to hoard tasks and chores because they feel like they have to please everyone around them or show everyone that they can do it all, but we're not down for that life sentence.

I'm not going to let you be doomed to constantly taking on more than you can reasonably handle all while always giving yourself the short end of the stick. It's okay to let people carry their own dirty laundry sometimes rather than you always feeling like you have to be the person to come along and step in to fix everything for everyone. You are not a handyman for people's lives, you are just one damn person, and you need to start giving your own self some of that time that you have been so overly generously giving away to everyone else.

As you start giving tasks, roles, or commitments away and giving them back, make a clear boundary so people know not to try to put anything like that on you again. No need to do it in a mean way, but just communicate in such a way that they know that you are no longer a go-to option for that sort of thing. And in the future, make sure that you are no longer going to take on the task of doing things for other people unless you genuinely want to, *and* have the mental capacity to. People can't just dump their to do lists onto your to do list because they are too damn lazy or tired to do things themselves. You are entitled to some free space, and you have a right to say no, and you need to start exercising that right. You are not the only person capable of doing many of the things that you feel so desperately need to get done. Somebody else can do it. Make like a business, and delegate, delegate, delegate.

Prioritize Your Life

Now that you have cut things out and delegated where you can, you should be left with a much more manageable list of commitments and things to do. Yay! This means fewer things to decide and more headspace to ruminate on life's most important decisions. So at this point, all you need to do is look at the priority of what is left on your list and start taking action towards getting it done. Make sure that you are clear on what is most important to you, as well as what is time sensitive so that you are getting everything done by its deadline and in order of what actually matters. Alternatively, if deadlines are not as pressing, you can start tackling your list by going for the things that have been weighing on you most heavily. This will often mean starting with the most stressful things or the things that have been on your list for the longest amount of time.

JUST FRICKIN PICK ONE   133

It is important that even after you have prioritized your current to do list, you continue to look through it and keep it prioritized. Start setting boundaries for yourself around what you are willing to add to your list and what you are not willing to add so that you are no longer being overwhelmed by too many tasks. You do not want to find yourself going through all of this work to clean up your time and tasks, only to find yourself having to recommit to doing it all over again because you have totally screwed it up again. Instead, allow yourself to be far more honest with yourself and those around you about what you actually care about. In other words, if your coworker's son is having his third birthday party and you can't stand the ill-behaved little brat, and you'd much rather clean your house...or stick needles in your eyes, don't go to the party. *Decide against it.* It is your right to decide to live your life for yourself, and no one can or should make you feel bad for wanting to do things your way rather than their way.

Make It Easier

Lastly, with what is left on your to do list and your regular schedule, look to see if you can make any of it easier. You don't have to just outsource to people, you can outsource to robots...kind of. Basically, you just want to find ways that you can use technology, software, apps, or electronics to streamline and simplify things you have to get done. Sometimes it's the big things that can trip us up, but sometimes, it's the little things accumulated together.

If you set your home's thermostat on a timer, that's one less thing for you to do, but more importantly, one less thing for you to think about and one less decision for you to have to make. As a matter of fact, it's many decisions you no longer have to make. Now you don't have to decide when to change the temperature, what to change it to, whether you're going to go upstairs to change it or go down the hallway, or whether you're going to tell your housemate or not that you changed it. That may seem like a small, insignificant thing. But remember, it's not just about the thing itself. It's about getting as much off your plate as possible and freeing mental space so you can have thinking room and mental capacity to make choices about the things that matter.

Another great way to simplify your life and make things easier is by batching. This entails doing like tasks all at the same time so that you can get them done faster. For example, if you need to go to the post office, drop some things off at the second-hand store, and go grocery shopping, do these tasks all in one single trip so that you do not have to make multiple separate trips later on. This way, you are only going out once instead of multiple times. If you have to go to the doctor, get your toes waxed, and get a haircut, book your appointments around the same time on the same day so you can knock everything out at once. Check all your emails at the same 1-2 hour window each day. Cook your meals for the week one day a week.

Every time we go to do a new task, there are mental switches that your brain needs to make that scatter your mental energy and harm your focus and concentration. And you've introduced a new activity that your brain needs to make a decision on. It now needs to decide what to do, when to do it, and how to do it. Batching can help eliminate some of this mental switching and combat decision fatigue so your brain doesn't get too tired of making choices around the little things and has the capacity to actually make choices around the big things.

CHAPTER 13

THE DOUCHEBAG IN YOUR HEAD

YOU KNOW that ridiculous little voice in your head that is constantly rattling off about the "What if"s and the "Maybe"s and the "Yeah, but"s? The one that says "What if I fail?" or "I'm not good enough to pull this off" or "What if I do the wrong thing?" That nasty little voice that is constantly crapping all over your parade, peeing on your ice cream cone, and stealing your potential joy because it keeps you paralyzed, in desperate fear that you're going to screw everything up? That voice is a complete ass. Also, that voice is you.

It's a tough pill to swallow, but that nasty bully that you have been holding on to in your mind was developed by you, and it exists only to serve you with information on behalf of the devil's advocate. Unfortunately, it rarely serves up the information in a reasonable (or kind) way, and it is notoriously unreliable when it comes to fact-checking its information and providing you with anything that has true merit to it. In most cases, that nasty voice has picked up slices of information from here and there, and it continues to spit it out at you on a regular basis regardless of if the information is actually true or complete or not.

At the heart of it, it means well. That voice wants to protect you from doing anything that is going to get you bullied, ridiculed, shamed, or dead. It wants what's best for you. It wants to keep you from experiencing pain, and keep you from experiencing death...literal death, but also figurative death of the person you once were, or the person you are now. With each decision comes change, and change means death. Now, we're talking about the big decisions here, not the *what am I going to eat for dinner* decisions. A decision to do something different, go somewhere different, pursue something different, become something different means that some part of you is going to die. But while that voice keeps you from experiencing loss and pain, it unfortunately keeps you from experiencing joy. That voice is like a brick wall. Sure, you keep the bad guys out, but it keeps the good guys out too.

You're so used to listening to that voice that you genuinely believe what it says to be true every time it speaks. And you trust it because you know it just wants to save you from heartache and pain. Still, that voice is a complete toxic jerk, and it needs to be taught a lesson and be put in its place so that it stops sabotaging everything you set out to do in life. Listening to that voice too closely or believing in everything it says is just a ticket to nowheresville in your life.

If you were on a road trip with someone who was constantly in your ear about everything that was wrong with you and everything that could go wrong with your life, would you just let them keep going on and on? Your life is that road trip. And that obnoxious Negative Nancy is the jerk in your head. You need to open that door, give it a swift kick, and turn that thing into road kill.

Ditching the douchebag in your head takes time and practice. You have to consider the fact that it has been living rent-free in your head for years, and that it has been your most trusted advisor and the voice of "reason" in your brain. Despite the fact that there have probably been times that you knew this voice was being unreasonable and was screwing you over, you stayed loyal to your toxic relationship and let it control you and your life outcomes in countless scenarios. It's time to kick that sucker out. No more squatting. It's time to regain control over your mind.

Nice Little Douchebag

That negative voice in your head is known as your survival instinct, and it is designed to recognize every possible negative outcome in your life and avoid the shit out of it. Your inner douchebag does not want to see you sad, crying, angry, hurt, or losing out on anything that makes you happy in life. So, instead of allowing the outer world to get you down and expose you to stress, that well-meaning douchebag exposes you to its own level of stress so that you do not go out and get hurt.

So instead of getting rejected by a potential date that you are interested in, you will talk yourself out of going in the first place so that potential love interest never gets the chance to hurt you. The logic here is that if you are the one sabotaging yourself, you might hurt yourself, but it will certainly not hurt nearly as much as someone else hurting you. And instead of risking getting caught off guard by a situation going down the tubes, and you potentially being confronted with a situation where you don't know what to do, you can just throw that situation down the tubes yourself on your own terms, therefore, you get to continue to feel in control. Better to know when the end is near so you can mentally and emotionally prepare for it.

Sounds logical, right? It would be if there was always a guarantee for the shit to hit the fan in every potential scenario. But luckily, that's not the case in life. In fact, the opposite is often true. This voice in your head assumes that you are going to get rejected or hurt every single time, when in reality, you are likely not going to be rejected or hurt nearly as often as you might think. In fact, if you give things a chance, you'll discover that more things work than don't. If you continue to assume that every single situation is going to turn out badly, however, then you're going to talk yourself out of every potential good thing in life. You are literally signing up for serving yourself crap on a platter, all day, every day. So, no matter how well-meaning it may be, when left unchecked, that inner douchebag can become far more destructive than any other douchebag out in the world.

Because of that survival instinct, we're so quick to ask ourselves, "What if it doesn't work?" And we never ever stop to ask the opposite question, "What if it does?" We always ask "What if it goes wrong?" But we never ask "What if it goes right?" Here's a new trick for an old dog— that's you, you're the old dog. Every time you get to one of those life decisions that feels big and scary because it can potentially alter the course of your life, start getting into the habit of asking yourself these new questions. Take the default negative questions and turn them around into their positive opposite.

Yeah, Yeah, Yeah…

Do you have a friend who overexaggerates everything, is always in a crisis, or is always freaking out about some situation or another? Every time they tell one of their stories, you kind of half listen, and nod along without really paying attention or taking what they're saying too seriously. Do you have a friend like that? If you answered yes, my condolences. If you are that friend, then you've got some serious work to do. And if you answered no, then you are wrong. Because we all have that friend. And it lives inside our heads. Allow me to reintroduce you to your survival instinct. Now, going back to your ridiculously overdramatic friend, how seriously would you take the things they say? Not very. You just shrug it off. You don't go making your life decisions based on the fictitious foolery that is coming out of their overdramatic mouth. But you do it all the time with the voice in your head.

Know that the key to collaborating with your inner voice is to stop taking everything it says so damn seriously. Listen, if that situation that it is comparing every other situation to happened more than ten years ago, resulted in no more than a skinned knee, and you have had many harmless encounters since then, the self-abuse and overwhelming fear you've been putting yourself through are completely unnecessary. You have plenty of evidence that what you are worried about is going to go just fine, so whatever it is, you should be perfectly capable of making the decision around it with ease, yet here you are still being influenced by this archaic mental monster that conveniently refuses to look at the statistics.

You can listen to what it is telling you—you should, it is a survival instinct after all, it's there for a reason. But, it doesn't always get the last word. Your logic and reason do. When you are faced with a choice, see what your survival instinct is pointing out to you, recognize what it is trying to protect you against, and now let your logic step in and take over to aid you in making your ultimate decision. Remember those questions for making decisions in Chapter 6? Use 'em. And seek guidance from a wise mentor if needed. But don't let that voice in your head have the last word, unchecked.

Do Shut Up

I had a friend who used to do this thing where they would always complain about the temperature. They'd always say, "It's hot. I'm hot." There's two problems with this. One—I don't care. And two—of course it's hot, it's 110 degrees, so why does that even need to be said? Eventually, this person realized, likely after a drastic reduction in their number of friends, that complaining about how hot it was didn't make it any cooler. And if they stopped complaining for a second, maybe they could actually think of a solution. But nooooo, their mind was too busy being filled and preoccupied with complaining about the problem...and annoying the crap out of their former friends in the process.

It's bad enough that the voice in your head not only makes it hard for you to make choices by incessantly pointing out the potential fatal downside to everything, but to make matters worse, it also has to complain. When it comes time to face a choice, complaining about how hard it is, how unfair it is, or how confusing it is will only lead to you feeling like the situation is even harder, more unjust, or more confusing than it actually is. Now, you start psyching yourself out, and not in a good way. The more you reinforce this dread over the decision-making process and the more negative words you use to characterize it, the more you start to convince yourself and your brain to genuinely believe these things, making it even harder on yourself to choose. Plus, you've now clouded your brain with both unreasonable pessimism, and now also dread and self-pity. How do you think you're going to come to a decision now?

Any time you find yourself complaining about your choices that need to be made, take it as an opportunity to play a game of the ol' mental switcheroo by reframing your complaints and choosing to see the decision in a more empowering light. Rather than seeing it as something to complain about, see it as something worth celebrating. You can revel in the fact that you have two great options to choose from, or the fact that you have a growth opportunity on your hands. The more decisions you make, the better you'll get at it and the easier and faster it will be for you. So go out there tiger, and get your head in the game, and get excited every time you have the opportunity to get some more practice under your belt.

Don't Jump Off The Train Too Soon

Now that you've conquered Negative Nancy and Complaining Cathy, the only giant left to slay is Doubting Dan.

It's done. You've made your choice. And now you wait to see how it plays out. But wait—you can't wait because you're driving yourself absolutely bonkers obsessing over the choice you just made. Be honest with yourself: how many times have you sat around your house moping about a decision that you made, questioning if it was right, and bullying yourself if you suddenly changed your mind and decided that it was wrong? The more you allow that voice to tell you that you have done everything wrong, the harder your life is going to feel and the more you are going to live with the pain of regret because you never saw anything through long enough to let it work out. Not to mention, you are also diminishing your trust and confidence in yourself by this constant questioning, and you'll be second guessing every single decision you make in the future, whether big or small potato.

If you were in Atlanta and you were riding on a train to Philadelphia, 800 miles away, and you got off too soon before the actual stop of your destination, you wouldn't get to where you wanted to go. If you got off somewhere in North Carolina, you can't complain that it ain't Philly. The train was trying to get you to your destination, but you jumped off too early, and now you're complaining about where you ended up and acting as if it's the train that's the issue. The train is your decision. The right train will get you to your desired goal, but if you get off the train too soon (ie, don't see your decision through long enough), you'll never get to where you want to go (the desired outcome of your choice). And it's not the train (the decision) that's the problem. The problem is you second guessing and not following through. Don't jump off the train too soon.

So are you ready to take on the task of seeing things through and cleaning up what you're saying to yourself after you have already made a choice? Good. Cancel out the noise of self-doubt. If it's a decision like most others, you can remind yourself that it is reversible or fixable down the line if you really need to change course. And if you assure yourself that you've made the best decision you could possibly make with the information available to you at the time, you can empower yourself to stand firm and confident in your choices. Then there's also the added benefit of no longer calling yourself names like a whiny little b-word or an idiot who never does anything right, so you'll start to feel better about yourself in general.

CHAPTER 14

PUT A RING ON IT

IT'S time to grow a pair and learn to commit for real.

Commitment is a word that can freak many people out (just ask my ex-boyfriend), often because they are viewing commitment with the wrong frame of mind. Too many people believe that committing to something means taking it on for life, like the commitment we make in marriage. In reality, commitment is nothing that we have to tie ourselves to forever. You are allowed to commit to something...*for now*.

You can take this as far as you want. I'm not trying to tell you to get married *for now*...and keep your options open and continue window shopping with a ring on your finger and a spouse on your arm. This is not to tear down the sanctity of marriage. I'm just saying that *every* commitment is not a blood oath, so every decision that leads to that temporary commitment doesn't have to feel like one. Children flit about from one stimulus to the next, never sticking to any one thing. And unfortunately with the help of social media, the internet, regular media, and the dopamine intoxication they cause, most children don't even have a chance to outgrow that behavior. Healthily functioning adults make commitments. They make decisions and stick to them.

As a matter of fact, maybe it's the definition of the word commitment we need to change. No, we're not going to write a petition to *Webster's,* but let's change the way we think of the word. Rather than viewing commitment as some death sentence that comes with a good old-fashioned ball and chain, try viewing commitment as a word that means "focus." When you commit to something, you are choosing to place your focus on it for the time being. If you decide to change your commitment later on, then all that means is that you are choosing to adjust your focus to rest somewhere else instead.

Reframing your meaning of commitment to mean focus rather than a lifetime sentence to your choice means that you can start seeing picking a decision as something that is more palatable, while at the same time giving you enough mental conviction to move forward and not stay stuck. So now, rather than committing to owning a pack of mountain fresh mint gum for the rest of your life, you can commit to just owning it for the rest of the pack and then getting a new flavor later if you decide that mountain fresh isn't really your minty preference.

Spoiler Alert: It's Probably Going To Work Out

How do I know that? How can I be so sure? How can I be

such a naive, positive Pollyanna? You're still alive right now, reading this book, so all the decisions you've made up until this point have at least been good enough for you to not totally crash and burn. So if you've been squinting your eyes, clenching your fists, and bracing for impact, waiting for your life to go south as a result of every decision that you make, chances are you are wasting *a lot* of your energy on literally nothing.

Most of the time, the things that we decide on or commit to end up being perfectly fine and we find that we are pleased with the outcome of our choices. You are a lot better at making decisions than you think you are. Once you recognize that most of the time it works out just fine, and realize that you actually do not suck completely at choosing things, your insides no longer have to churn every time you have to pick something. Then, you can feel way more confident in committing to your decisions, seeing them through, and allowing them the chance to turn into a positive result.

Look at your track record of decision making. Like I said, you're still alive, so you get brownie points there. And if you look a little deeper on everything you've done, you'll find that you've likely made plenty of great choices in your lifetime. You just haven't been regularly paying attention to those outcomes and using them to help you build confidence in yourself. So instead of beating yourself up over present decisions and diminishing your confidence, praise yourself for past decisions to bolster your confidence for the choice you have to make in front of you now. Think of all the positive moments and opportunities and experiences that gave you enjoyment or pride. Then think about the decision you had to make in order to make those moments a reality.

And Then What?

Here's a little game that can help you step beyond the fear of everything hitting the fan. Here's how you play. It's easy. You just ask yourself "And then what?" after you think about what could go wrong with a choice. The results often look something like this: (Bear with me, yes, this will be another food example because, as you've probably noticed, I am eternally hungry.)

"What if I order this meal and it sucks?"

"And then what?"

"I have a meal that I do not like."

"And then what?"

"I finish it. Or I don't."

"And then what?"

"I go home and make Pop-Tarts. I love Pop-Tarts."

As you can see, in this decision, nothing horrible happened. No nuclear war, no global pandemic, no waterboarding. You learned that you can just make a decision, enjoy it if it works, and easily correct course by choosing an alternative if it doesn't work. Sure, you may be out the cash that the meal cost you, but consider it a small fee for learning something about yourself and learning information that can help you make that choice or one like it again in the future.

Say Yes To Yourself Today, Say Thank You To Yourself Tomorrow

When it comes to ditching your decision commitment phobia, it is always a good idea to just remember that when everything does work out in the end, which it always does, you are going to feel amazing. Think back to every time that you have made a decision, and it worked out in your favor, and you felt amazing because the results were exactly what you were looking for. What if you had been too afraid to commit to those choices? What if you were such a wuss that when it came to saying yes to those opportunities, instead you said no and robbed yourself of the opportunity to engage in those experiences? Imagine if you had say no because you were so afraid of everything going wrong that you decided you just couldn't do it? Then, rather than having the chance to experience something totally amazing and potentially life-changing, you missed out entirely. Instead of having a great experience followed by an amazing memory, you simply had another notch in your belt from yet another time that you were too chicken shit to say yes. How disappointing would that be? Wouldn't that have sucked?

Robbing yourself of the chance to have awesome things happen to you because of a fear of commitment is weak, bro. Stop holding yourself back because you're too scared to say yes, and start opening yourself up to the fullness of life by bucking up and saying yes. Fast forward to one day, when you're old and wrinkly and showing your grandkids a scrapbook of your life:

"Grandma, why's it empty?"

"Because, little Billy, I was too afraid to commit to any decision, so I never did anything."

"But Grandma, does that make you sad?"

"No, Billy. I got all the way through life unscathed and unharmed."

"Looks like you didn't really live life at all."

"Well, my heart's still beating isn't it? Everything worked out. None of the bad things happened."

"But Grandma, none of the good things happened either—"

"Shut up, Billy, go upstairs, it's past your bedtime."

See, even your future grandson is wise enough to know that saying yes to things and committing to decisions is a roadmap for a life well-lived with no regrets.

The End Is Not Near

Have you ever had this dreadful feeling like your whole life would end if something did not work out because so much was riding on it? As humans, we do this strange thing where we have weirdly exaggerated fears around our decisions because we're afraid that everything is going to go so horribly that we simply won't survive. Perhaps you were preparing for a first date with someone, and as the time got closer and closer, you grew more and more petrified, convinced that everything would go wrong. Or maybe you had a first day at work, and you got extremely anxious, convinced that your boss would see you for the screw up you really are and publicly fire you before you even have enough time to put that framed picture of your mother and your cat on your new desk. Maybe you had to do or say something in front of a crowd, and you convinced yourself you'd bomb it and never be able to live it down. Having these fears is normal. But it's also complete bullshit.

Listen, no one died because they had a terrible date with someone, nor did they die because they got something wrong on their first day at a new job. In fact, most of the things that you are terrified of in your life are not going to do anything beyond possibly cause some temporary mental discomfort in your life. Think about it: if your date goes so horribly, you can always excuse yourself early and go home, then laugh it off with a friend, start a dating blog on your misadventures, and one of your blog posts goes viral, leading you to get a book deal, and your book ends up on the New York Times bestseller list, catching the attention of Oprah, who uses it as one of her favorite things, making you an instantaneous multi-millionaire overnight. Hey, if you're going to be so ridiculous and aim for the stars with how horribly everything could potentially go, you might as well use that same energy to aim for the stars with how well it could go.

In most cases, even when things go wrong, they don't go so horribly wrong that your pulse will stop. As much as we feed into this fear and let our minds get away from us, the everyday situations that we find ourselves worrying about are not nearly as dangerous as we make them out to be. Trust me: no matter how uncomfortable a situation may be, you are going to survive it. When it comes to your decisions, sometimes their outcomes can lead to different results than what you had in mind, but it doesn't mean they can't still work out in your favor. So say yes to opportunities, say yes to life, just pick a direction, and go for it.

See Your Silver Linings In Advance

Another great way to combat your intense fear is to think about what you are going to learn and what experiences you are going to have if everything goes terribly wrong. In most cases, everything we go through, even if it ends up being crappy, can bring some form of joy or knowledge to our lives. Softies call this "finding the silver lining." You have to have the belief that no matter what happens, it's not all bad, and there will be something to learn or to celebrate.

If you are having a hard time staying committed to a choice, you can think about all of the things that you can count as silver linings before you even engage in the commitment. For example, if you want to start a new business, but you are terrified that you are going to fail, you can think about all the things that you will gain from even giving it a shot in the first place. You could pay attention to the fact that you will gain the experience of running a business and you can always transfer those skills over to a regular job if you have to. Or, you could acknowledge that you are bound to learn some great skills about self-management, leadership, and your industry of choice.

No matter what ultimately happens with your business, you are bound to learn plenty of useful information and acquire many valuable skills that you can use to help you in ventures later in life. There are virtually no experiences in life that are devoid of lessons or joy, so never allow yourself to fall into the belief that you have nothing to gain from any choice you make. One way or another, you are going to learn something about yourself or about life that will keep you growing forward and feeling more confident about yourself and all that you have to offer.

At the end of the day, everything in life is about learning or experiencing. Making decisions, and even refusing to make decisions and staying in limbo, contributes to all that you learn and all that you gain in this lifetime. The more that you commit to things, the more you'll learn, the more value you'll get from life, and the more you'll enjoy the ride. Eventually, you will find that you truly have nothing to lose in most cases so you may as well go ahead and make the decisions that will ultimately bring you wisdom and happiness.

If The Shit *Really* Hits The Fan, Know This

In the event that an outcome is truly horrible, it is important that you learn how to acknowledge this as an important life lesson all the same. Sometimes, you are going to decide on something, and the outcome is going to be bad, and extremely challenging for you to own and face. In these rare situations, you may encounter trauma, tragic loss, extreme shame, or other experiences that are dreadful and painful. Fortunately, these are extremely rare situations, so there is no need to go through everyday life as if every choice you make will result in this level of outcome. However, this is often the very reason why we are so damn scared to make a move in the first place: we do not want to experience a huge loss in our lives. Chances are you have a few of these under your belt already, which is why you are so afraid to encounter them again and you're so petrified to choose something in the first place.

It is important to realize that in addition to being very rare, these such outcomes can also be healed. Often, the way to heal is by being intentional about the decisions that you make afterward, properly accepting and processing the emotions that followed your original decision, and allowing time to do its thing. And if necessary, do not be afraid to reach out for support. Arming yourself with friends, family, and even therapists can be a great way to help you come to terms with what the outcome of your decision was and recognize that it was an unlikely scenario that is not likely to happen again. Over time, you can rebuild your confidence and trust in yourself to prevent you from feeling terrified of making the same mistake all over again, which could potentially set you back into a state of indecisiveness. If something like this is the reason why you are so indecisive now, go through the aforementioned healing steps so you can move beyond the challenges that you are facing and forgive yourself and move forward in your life.

CHAPTER 15

PRACTICE MAKES YOU SUCK LESS

ARE you confident doing a donut in the snow in a formula one car? Are you confident walking across a ¾ inch wide wire between two skyscrapers with no net below you? How do you feel about controlling a 175,000 pound machine carrying 416 people at 35,000 feet in the air? If you're not a professional race car driver, a tightrope walker, or a pilot, you probably said no thanks to all three. And why did you say no? Because you haven't done those things a million times like the people who get paid to professionally do those things have. Do you think Tony Hawk was confident the very first time he did a two-and-a-half aerial spin on a skateboard? Nope. But the more he did it, the more confident he got. Your decisions are the same way.

When you practice making decisions over and over again on a regular basis, you build up your confidence in yourself and in your decision-making skills. If you want to stop sucking so damn much at making choices in your life, practice is going to be the way. Not only will you build confidence, but you'll strengthen the logic and the logical process that you use to make choices in the first place, which will make future choices quicker and easier to make.

Practicing making decisions can be done three different ways, and depending on how badly you think your decision-making confidence needs a boost, you can choose how much energy you want to put into getting your practice in and which method is most suited for you. You can either practice with the decisions you already make in your regular day to day life, go out of your way to try new things and force yourself to confront new decision-making challenges, or you can play games that force you to make and commit to decisions.

If you only want to practice with your day to day, run of the mill choices, all you have to do is take the choices you make on a daily basis, and force yourself to make the same types of choices faster. Instead of spending ten minutes figuring out what you're going to eat, spend five minutes, and gradually get that decision-making time down lower and lower. The aim here is to get you to start thinking faster and get used to committing to choices faster. We're trying to get Parkinson's law to work in our favor.

Alternatively, you can also take your day to day decisions, and try making different choices around them. If you always wear the blue shirt, pick the red one. The idea here is to show yourself that you can make a decision that is different than what you would normally choose and it can still turn out okay. On a deeper level, you are gaining confidence in the idea that there is more than one "right" way to do something, and more than one way to get to a positive result, the realization of which will eventually lead to you having much less anxiety over picking things.

The next way is to throw yourself into the fire. No, not literally. Don't do that. And definitely don't tell your lawyer I told you to. I mean, try something totally new and different for you. It can be a new skill, a new sport, or a new hobby. Whatever this new thing is, it will come with tons of micro decisions that will need to be made along the way in order to ensure the successful execution of it, so it'll be a great way to strengthen your decision-making muscle, while also exercising it in a way and in an environment that it's not used to. And any lessons learned can be applied to how you make choices in other areas of your life.

And thirdly, for the fun way, you can always start playing games that require you to decide. Things like mazes or puzzles, or anything where you have to pick what way to go or what you are going to try to do in order to create the outcome that you desire, can be a great opportunity for you to build your decision-making skills because you have to pick one thing, and see the outcome through. You'll find that in some cases, your decisions will be right, and they will get you where you wanted to go, and in other cases, your decision will have been wrong, and you will find yourself needing to correct your mistake. But you'll find that 9 times out of 10, you get to where you want to go even if there were a few detours along the way.

Games are a fun way to start learning how to confidently make and commit to your choices, and also come to terms with the fact that sometimes your choices will be wrong. In these instances, you'll see how to handle things when they do turn out wrong, or different than planned. You'll realize that the outcome of your mistakes is not tragic and catastrophic, and there's no need to feel like a total failure because you made an oopsies. Your errors were quickly and easily correctable, as is the case with most real-life decisions as well.

If mazes and logic puzzles make you feel like you're a nine-year-old on a road trip to Grandma's, maybe a game of "would you rather" is more your speed. How can choosing between licking peanut butter off a stranger's toe and pole dancing on the subway help you make better choices? Even something as ridiculous as this will help you learn about what kind of reasoning you use to make your decisions and will force you to dig deep for reasons as to why you make your ultimate choice, giving you practice in weighing options and projecting consequences.

And while we're on the subject, now I'm curious:

Would you rather lick peanut butter off a stranger's toe or pole dance on the subway?

Oh, you're gross.

Pay Attention To The Obvious

JUST FRICKIN PICK ONE   161

Remember when I said, there were three main ways you can practice making better choices? Well, there's actually a fourth. I under-promised and now I'm overdelivering. You're welcome. Another way to help you get better at making decisions and practice strengthening the logic involved in your decision-making process is to bring intentional decision making into your daily life—that is bring extra awareness to the process by which you come to decide about things.

Each time you have a small decision come up, such as which yoga mat to get from Amazon or whether or not you should say yes to that blind date invitation, slow down and walk through the process of making your choice. Even if it's something seemingly small where you make your choice quickly, do this. In fact, it's better if you practice this with something you're used to choosing easily. Break it down. Tell yourself what questions you're asking and what general goals you're prioritizing to help you come to your choice. You're probably going to feel like an idiot for doing all of this thinking over whether you should watch a movie or binge watch a show, or whether you should dye your hair red or black. But the idea is to uncover the reasoning behind your choices so you can use it as a framework and apply that reasoning to other choices that may not be so quick and automatic for you.

Even though this exercise may seem pointless, you want to use it to train your brain to understand the steps involved in deciding so that it automatically recognizes them and begins moving through them with less obvious choices. The more you practice this, the more chance you give your brain to automatically call on these steps to help you get through other forks in the road. And the more you gain insight into information about yourself that can help you make the bigger decisions.

Pull Out Your Pom Poms

If you're going to become the superstar athlete of decision making, you know what you need? Cheerleaders. Have you ever been to a basketball game that did not have cheerleaders? What about a football game without cheerleaders? Nope. Cheerleaders are powerful because they bring energy to what's happening. They help the players build their confidence, and they are positive reinforcement that the players are doing good and are on the right track, which makes them want to keep up the good work. Cheerleaders fill the silence that would otherwise be filled with self-doubt and self-deprecation, with sounds of joy, optimism, and encouragement. Cheerleaders are just as essential to the game as the players on the field are. Cheerleaders for president! Sorry. Too far. Can you tell that I used to be a cheerleader?

My point is: you need to be your own cheerleader. Do not be afraid to cheer yourself on every time you make a great choice that turns out well. You can even go so far as to treat yourself by going to the spa, or going to your favorite restaurant...as long as you don't start sweating bullets when you have to decide between a deep tissue massage or shiatsu, or chicken or surf and turf. But having awesome results from a choice that you made is not the only reason to celebrate. It's also a win worth celebrating if you find yourself making progress towards making decisions faster or easier.

This way, you'll be building optimism and hope around your decisions instead of pessimism and anxiety. This'll alleviate stress and pressure around filtering future options, and build trust in the fact that you and the old thinker between your ears can actually make good choices. So put on that pleated skirt, pull out those pom poms, and get ready to hip hip hooray your way to a well-deserved pat on the back for your progress. But maybe just metaphorically. Or at least not in public.

CONCLUSION

Making decisions can be damn hard, can't it? From having to sort through the details, to figuring out what it is that you really want and then owning and committing to that decision, it can truly be a lot. Seriously, though, we have a tendency to put way more pressure on our decisions than is necessary, which can make the process even more challenging than it needs to be. Don't get me wrong, some choices are challenging, and you are going to have a hard time determining which option you need to choose. You may feel obligated to do what someone else wants you to do because you want to make them feel happy or control their perception of you. You may also want to avoid feeling regret or disappointment in yourself, which causes worry, fear, and stress to kick in.

If you haven't picked up on it already, one of the biggest reasons why people struggle to make decisions is because they lack self-confidence. This can arise for many reasons, and when it comes to bigger potatoes, this can cause many different problems in your life. Maybe you grew up with one or more assholes telling you that you are unworthy of having good things in life. This can cause you to subconsciously self-sabotage and believe that you are unworthy of picking things that make you happy. But you're not a complete masochist, and you know you don't want to be *un*happy, so you'll struggle with making the opposite decision as well.

Or maybe you lack confidence in your decision-making skills because you never learned how to make healthy decisions in the first place, so you often find yourself making poor choices and facing unwanted consequences as a result. Regularly facing unwanted consequences from low-quality decision-making skills can lead any average person to feel totally incapable, and afraid to make any choice at all for fear of making the wrong one. Growing past any level of low self-confidence that you may be dealing with can power boost your decision-making skills, making it a lot easier for you to choose without excess fear or anxiety. Once you alleviate this type of fear, you will be surprised to see just how fast you get with choosing because you are no longer facing two choices every single time: the one at hand and the decision to either choose what makes you happy or choose what you think you deserve.

Permission to be woo woo for a moment: perhaps the most rewarding part of all this is that if you implement what's in this book, using the same tools you use to become more adept at making decisions, you'll have the added benefit of getting to know yourself, which is essential for creating and living a life that you love. As part of your self-discovery, you'll also uncover and debunk the damaging mental beliefs that hold you back and contribute to your decision anxiety in the first place. And remember, everything becomes easier with confidence and practice. But practice doesn't mean perfect. And it doesn't have to.

Tap into your willingness to accept yourself when things don't turn out as planned, and find a way to be kind towards yourself regardless of what mistakes you make or what difficulties you face. If you have been unkind to yourself at any point in the past due to the outcomes of past decisions, be kind to yourself now by forgiving yourself for that and being willing to learn how to do better going forward. This will release you to build confidence in your ability to make good choices for the future. The more kind you are to yourself about your weaknesses and your losses, the easier it will be for you to recognize your strengths and your wins and continue to build on them, so that you can trust yourself even more. When it comes to strength building, you'll find the simple act of treating yourself with kindness to be very helpful in building your trust in yourself and cementing the genuine belief that you have what it takes to make the right decisions and do the right things.

But building strength and making huge decisions with ease doesn't happen right off the bat. Think about it this way: if someone asked you to pick up a 300 pound barbell right now, do you think you could do it? Probably not, unless you are some Hulk-sized bodybuilder, in which case, pick another metaphor. But for those of you who are average like me, chances are a huge barbell like that would be impossible to pick up on the first try. You would not trust yourself to be able to do it because you've never done it successfully in the past, therefore you could not trust your mind or body to be able to carry that much weight reasonably. However, if you were to spend time building your muscles and learning how to carry weights, over time you would find that a 300 pound barbell may be nothing for you because you have built up your strength enough to be able to lift it. Handling big decisions is the same way.

And remember, you're not alone in all this. No, I'm not talking about the other hundreds of millions of strangers in the world who are screwballs who break a sweat in the McDonald's drive-thru line just like you used to do before reading this book. Although, sure you can take comfort in that too. But I'm talking about the people who are closest to you. You either already have or can seek out and gain the wisdom, knowledge, and comfort from people who have gone through what you're going through to help you figure out the best future course of action for you. You may think you have an impossible decision before you, but no matter what you're facing and how difficult or impossible it may seem to make sense of it, there is someone else who has been where you are, and with the help of a series of right decisions, made it out the other side. While your choices are ultimately up to you, don't forget that you're not alone and if you get in a tough spot, it's okay to seek guidance from outside resources that may be able to see your blindspots.

The caveat, however, is that you are very intentional about who your resources are. As alluded to previously, it is not helpful for you to seek the counsel of people who have different values than you, as these individuals will end up showing you perspectives that may be irrelevant to what actually matters most to you in your life. While an expanded perspective is always helpful, avoid allowing people with wildly different viewpoints from you to persuade you to make decisions that do not align with your values. Ultimately, maintain your trust in yourself by acting in integrity with yourself regardless of what other people say about your situation, and don't let anyone dissuade you from your ultimate values, no matter how much you respect that person. Their job is not to make the decision for you. Their job is to show you any blindspots or present to you any information that you are not seeing that can make it easier for you to make the decision yourself. The choice is still yours.

And that's the thing about choices. You always have one. You have the choice to begin, you have the choice to continue, and you have the choice to stop. You always have a choice. Remembering this alone can take the edge off and make you more comfortable picking things without decision anxiety. Remember, you're not going to be joined in holy matrimony to your every decision until the end of time.

Fortunately, now, you have a reliable template that you can use to walk you through the decision-making process and reframe it so it doesn't seem so scary. You can also continue building your trust and confidence in yourself so that you can start to feel assured that the choices you make are the right ones for you and that you'll be strong enough to make them work in your favor in the long run. This will eliminate the need you feel to question yourself and replay things a thousand times over. So now instead of wasting all your time worrying and wigging out, you can make a decision and get on with your life already, knowing that you can always fix things or change course down the line if absolutely necessary.

Look at you. You're different. I can tell. You are turning into one lean, mean, turbo, decision-making machine. Look at that sparkle in your eye. I can see it. That's the sparkle of a quicker picker—someone who makes decisions, and makes them good and quick. That drive thru menu can't intimidate you. You're not phased by picking a new career change. Swiping through thousands of potential suitors on Tinder and securing dates with the top contenders? Easy. Nailing down a marketing plan at work? Cakewalk. Picking a new house? You make it look easier than *House Hunters*. You've got this, my little decision-making badass. Go out there and show the world your newfound ability to just frickin pick one.

LIKE WHAT YOU JUST READ?
PLEASE LEAVE A REVIEW ON AMAZON

If you enjoyed this book and feel empowered to take control over your life, I ask that you leave a review on Amazon.

Your feedback is greatly appreciated. Hearing your opinion and understanding how my (hopefully) inspiring experiences and understandings may help you improve your own life is valuable in helping me to continue producing great content to support you in living your best life.

Plus, it makes me smile inside to see I'm able to have a positive effect on someone else's life with my antics.

Thanks a million,

-Reese

ME, AGAIN...

Thanks a bunch for getting this book!

Sad that it's over?

Turn that frown upside down. If you don't want the fun to end, below are all the ebooks, paperback books, and audiobooks I have available on Amazon and Audible.

B*tch Don't Kill My Vibe:

How To Stop Worrying, End Negative Thinking, Cultivate Positive Thoughts, And Start Living Your Best Life

Just Do The Damn Thing:

How To Sit Your @ss Down Long Enough To Exert Willpower, Develop Self Discipline, Stop Procrastinating, Increase Productivity, And Get Sh!t Done

Make Your Brain Your B*tch:

Mental Toughness Secrets To Rewire Your Mindset To Be Resilient And Relentless, Have Self Confidence In Everything You Do, And Become The Badass You Truly Are

Chill Out, Bro:

How To Freak Out Less, Attack Anxiety, Calm Worry, & Rewire Your Brain For Relief From Panic, Stress, & Anxious Negative Thoughts

Milton Keynes UK
Ingram Content Group UK Ltd.
UKHW021933201124
451474UK00014B/1073

9 781951 238179